T0116860

MY
FATHER'S
BUSINESS

MY FATHER'S BUSINESS

DWAYNE LOPES

abbott press

Abbott Press books may be ordered through booksellers or by contacting:

Abbott Press
1663 Liberty Drive
Bloomington, IN 47403
www.abbottpress.com
Phone: 1 (866) 697-5310

ISBN: 978-1-4582-0061-7 (sc)
ISBN: 978-1-4582-0060-0 (e)

Library of Congress Control Number: 2011917571

Print information available on the last page.

Abbott Press rev. date: 03/08/2018

This book is passionately dedicated to God the Father for his only begotten Son Jesus the Christ through the Holy Spirit, and to my wife Maria, as well as my offspring's Richard, Dwayne Jr., and Diana.

CONTENTS

PREFACE

§ ξ

My Father's business is a very large and lucrative business that consists of a widely diverse ethical background of people that comes from all walks of life.

There is an estimate of two billion employees and growing that work inside and for the business. My father's business is the fastest growing business in the world in spite of a slow economy. My father established his business long before Bill Gates, Steve Jobs, Donald Trump, or Mark Zuckerberg were even born. My father's business is a fishing business, and it started out as a small entrepreneur business but rapidly grew because of the newly hired recruits into a large commercial fishing corporation. My father was very diligent in his business, for the bible declares in the book of Proverbs ch.22 verse 29, "See thou a man diligent in his business? He shall stand before kings".

My father has never stood before kings, but kings have stood and bowed before him, because he is the King of Kings and the Lord of Lords. The eternal blueprints of my father's business were designed by him in his creative imagination long time ago before the world began or was created. In the book of Revelation ch.4 verse 3, there is a resemblance referring to God who sits on the throne to look upon like a sardine stone which represents the logo sign for my father's organization.

The fish symbol that is encircle by a rainbow is placed on the door of the organization, but it does not only stand for God and God's abundant provision for his people, but also <u>Christian evangelism</u> to the lost and <u>edification</u> to the church body of many believers, and this is strictly my father's business.

Jesus said follow me and he would make us fishers of men. My father's fishing business is not for fun, pleasure, or a hobby for relaxation and enjoyment like most fishing trips, but it is a serious business. Men souls are at stake and the Bible states to win men souls over to the Lord Jesus one must be wise in doing so, for "He (or she) that wins souls is wise," (Proverbs ch.11 verse 30).

Some people consider fishing a water sport; however, it takes a lot of time and patience because one must first learn the art of fishing on how to catch the fish (which represents mankind's heart) before one can clean the fish entirely. Throughout the Bible Jesus sometimes referred to his faithful followers as sheep. I believe there are some similarities between people and sheep, and one of them are they both live on dry land. I also believe if people could not live on dry land, but they had to live in water Jesus probably would not refer to his followers as sheep but fish.

There are millions or billions of different kinds of fish in the seas, lakes, and oceans combined and most of them could easily represent humanity in a spiritual sense on planet earth. There is an estimate of seven billion people on the planet earth and statistically two billion are believe to be born again Christians worldwide.

However, many of them are ignorant when it comes to knowing the will or work of God for their own personal lives, for the exception of the chosen ones. Jesus said in the book of Matthew ch.20 verse 14 that "Many (people) are called, but only a few (people) are chosen."

The chosen ones not only know the will of God for their own lives, but help to educate others to discover the will or work of God for their lives as well. If you are wandering who the chosen ones are, I believe the chosen ones operate from the five different offices of ministry found in the book of Eph. ch.4 verse 11, which are Apostles, Prophets, Evangelists, Pastors, and Teachers, but what about the many that are called that Jesus refers to?

Question number one

1.) What are they (the many) called to do?
2.) What is the will or work of God the Father for their personal lives?
3.) What if you are not an Apostle, Prophet, Evangelist, Pastor, or Teacher?
4.) How would you discover the will of God for your life as one of the many that are called?
5.) What was the will of God the Father for his own son Jesus?
6.) Can believers complete the will of God in their lifetime before they die?
7.) Do you know the only ones that are going to heaven are the ones who do God's will or work?
8.) What is the difference between God's divine will and our own earthy will?
9.) Can or will a believer be punished by God knowing the will or work of God for their life but not do it?
10.) What is and what is not the will of God?

These series of questions require real Biblical practical answers which are located inside the King James Bible, and in the book of Jeremiah Ch. 33 verse 3, God said "Call unto me and I will answer you and show you great and mighty things that you know not" or you do not know.

It is the Spirit of God that led and instructed me to write this book, so the things which have been kept secret from the foundations of the world will be shared and revealed from the unseen invisible realm to our seen visible world. Through spiritual truths and natural concepts unto the lost children of unbelievers, babes, and adults in Christ that read it and want to know God's good, acceptable, and perfect will for their lives.

Not only to become fully enlightened, but to accomplish his will before departing earth and grow in grace from babes to spiritually developed mature adult believers. The spiritual reality of maturity is reflecting Jesus and becoming more like his Christ-like character with the fruits of the Spirit in our thoughts, (be)attitudes, and actions which takes a lifetime to build and to develop (Gal. ch.5 v.22-23).

As a young child, Jesus amazed many bright scholars in his day inside Herod's Temple and at the age of twelve years old, he stated to his earthly parents Joseph and Mary that "I must be about my Father's business." Eighteen years later after making this prophetic statement to his earthly parents, Jesus started his public ministry at the age of thirty. I believe the eighteen years that were unaccounted for of his personal life he was preparing and studying doing private ministry.

For before a person can preach or teach and perform open, honest and effective public ministry, he or she must make preparation in privacy. The beginning letter of F in Father is capitalized to show that Jesus was referring to his heavenly

(God) Father and not his earthly father Joseph. My Father's business can also be interpreted as "My Father's work" and or "My Father's will" which were both completed in a short three and a half year period of time by Jesus at the age of thirty-three which is a significant age. For when the number 33 is separated as individual numbers and becomes 3+3, it equals the number six. The number six in the Bible represents man, for man was created by God on the sixth day, so Jesus not only died as the Son of man, but for man (kind).

CHAPTER ONE

"Early Childhood Spiritual Education"

In the book of Jeremiah ch.1 verse 5, God said to the prophet Jeremiah "Before I formed thee (you) in (your mother's) belly, I knew thee (you) and before thou (you) came forth out of the womb I sanctified (set apart) thee (you), and I ordained thee (you) a prophet unto the nations." Jeremiah was a descendant from the Tribe of Benjamin who was born in a priestly family, in the town of Anatoth, but he was also known as a weeping prophet. He often shower a lot of his prophecies in tears of compassion. Some people categorized Jeremiah as one who showed his emotions quite often. One time, Jeremiah became emotionally discouraged and he wanted to retired from preaching the gospel.

But while he was pondering the decision, he realized God's word was like a blazing and combustible fire consuming his very soul. Jeremiah was and is still mainly remembered today in the church for saying God's word is like a liquid fire shut up or put up on the inside of his bones.

On the other hand, John the Baptist declared in the book of Matthew ch.3 verse 11 "that Jesus himself will baptize you with the Holy Ghost and with fire." If I ever preach this message somewhere in a pulpit, I would title it "Fireworks", and I'm not talking about the displaying of firecrackers in the night sky for 30 to 45 minutes on the 4th of July.

God told Jeremiah that he knew him before he was created in his mother's stomach, and in the book of Matthew ch.10 verse 30, "Jesus said the very hairs on the top of your head are all numbered by God." I am very amazed when I read this passage of scripture, because it is not just Jeremiah the prophet alone God is talking to or about here. God is also letting us know he knows everything and every detail of our life before he created us to inhabit the earth. Some of us already know according to Psalm 51 verse 5 that when we were conceived from our mother's womb we were born a sinner with a sinful nature and shaped in our iniquities.

Let's do a quick reference recap on how all of us came into existence in this state of condition. In the book of Genesis ch.2 verses 16 and 17, God commanded the first created man called Adam, "Of every tree of the garden thou (you) may freely eat, but of the tree of the knowledge of good and evil, thou (you) shall not eat of it; for in the day that thou (you) eat thereof thou (you) shall surely die."

In Genesis ch.3 verse 6, Eve (Adam's wife) was deceived by the devil serpent, and she ate the forbidden fruit and offered it to her husband, and he ate willfully and disobeyed God's direct command. This is a real valuable lesson here, for I believe most of the time women are deceived into sin while men on the other hand decides to sin in spite of God's commandments.

God said in his ten commandments, "Do not kill." Our federal and state prisons are filled with men and women who have killed. God said, "Do not steal", but some people steal regardless of what God said. God said, "Do not lie", for the devil or Satan himself is a liar, and the father of lies according to John ch.8 verse 44, but some men and women lie anyway. Why is this so? The answer is crystal clear and very simply from a Biblical standpoint. For our forefather Adam, and his one decision of disobedience to God's command brought into existence a fallen impure nature (which is basically several acts of disobedience to God's commandments) that replaced an innocent and pure nature from the out start of creation.

Furthermore, Adam had a freedom of choice (a free will) to obey God or disobey, for he was created as a free moral agent. However, God told Adam to choose wisely because in the day that he chose to eat of the forbidden fruit he would surely die according to the book of Genesis ch.2 verse 17.

Now, I often wonder was God speaking of a physical death or a spiritual death, eventually God spoke of both. The spirit world was first existing before the natural created world; therefore, Adam surely did die. He died an immediate spiritual death first through separation from God by eviction from the Garden of Eden and eventually he died a physical natural death second. Adam was spiritually dead, a walking physical zombie co-existing with God, a life quickening spirit in the natural earth realm of time. Because of Adam and Eve disobedience in the Garden of Eden, we not only lost our innocence and immortality, but we also lost our relationship and fellowship with God.

In the Garden of Eden, Adam and Eve lost everything, but in the Garden of Gethsemane Jesus prayed and made special preparation for us to gain everything back from what the enemy stole from us by victory of the cross. Adam can do nothing to revitalize his spirit within from the dead back to spiritual life except what Jesus stated in the book of John ch.3 verse 3 to Nicodemus (a learned teacher of religious law) "You must be born again!"

In other words, Adam and Nicodemus both had to be spiritually reborn, not only a rebirth of the spirit inside them, but born of water as well. Some Christians believe that born of water means to be born again by the Word of God.

However, I believe Jesus was signifying being born of water as taking the physical body and fully immerse it in physical natural water (known as the water of baptism). For Jesus himself was baptized by his cousin John the Baptist. I also believe in the renewal of spiritual birth which is receiving the fire baptism of the Holy Spirit. Remember what I said earlier, "Fireworks," but let's look and search deeper into the eternal scriptures to see what exactly is the Holy Ghost, and how does a believer receive the Holy Ghost plus what is the purpose for it.

First and foremost, the Holy Ghost is a gift from God, and a Comforter known as the Spirit of Truth according to John ch.15 verse 26. When the Spirit of Truth comes He (is a Spirit) will guide you into all truth, and he shall not speak of himself, but whatsoever things he shall hear that shall he speak, and he will show you things to come (John ch.16 verse 13).

Where does this precious gift come from and where will he live when he arrives? God said in the book of James ch.1 verse 17 that, "Every good gift and every perfect gift is from above, and comes down from the Father of lights. The Holy Spirit comes directly from heaven above and comes to live inside of you according to 1st Corinthians ch.6 verse 19. The Holy Ghost is a wonderful free gift sent by God, and gifts are freely given by one person (the giver of the gifts) to another person (the receiver or the recipient of the gifts) with no strings attached. Gifts are not earned but freely given out of love. If gifts are earned, it would not be a gift at all, but a deserving reward because of our own personal efforts. So once again, the Holy Ghost is a free gift given by God (the giver) and we are the Christian recipients of the gift.

How do we receive this gift from God? You simply ask God for it in prayer and wait patiently until he gives it to you. The bible states in the book of James ch.4 verse 2, "You have not, because you ask not".

In other words, you do not have the gift of the Holy Ghost, because you did not ask God for it in faith. Jesus declared in the book of Luke ch.11 verse 9-13, "Ask, and it shall be given you; seek, and you shall find; knock, and it shall be opened unto you." For <u>every one</u> that asks receive; and he that seeks finds, and to him that knocks it shall be opened. If a son shall ask bread of any of you that is a father, will he give him a stone? Or if he ask a fish, will he for a fish give him a serpent? Or if he shall ask an egg, will he offer him a scorpion? If you then, being evil, know how to give good gifts unto your children: how much more shall your (good) heavenly Father give the Holy Spirit to them that ask him?"

Jesus himself was baptized physically in the Jordan River by his cousin John the Baptist, and then his spirit was baptized spiritually by the Holy Ghost in the book of Matthew ch.3 verse 16. There really is no certain way or single method on how to receive the Holy Ghost, for I know some believers have received the Holy Spirit like the way Jesus did. After their physical bodies were baptize in water, immediately after when they came out of the water they receive the Holy Ghost. However, the book of Acts ch.10 verse 44 declares some Gentile believers receive the gift of the Holy Spirit before their physical bodies were immersed in natural water. I have heard some believers have received the Holy Ghost this way beforehand, and then they were baptized in water.

According to the book of Acts ch.19 verses 1-5 there were some believers in the city of Ephesus that were disciples of John the Baptist that were baptized by John with the baptism of repentance in the Jordan River. According to verse number two, they did not even hear at that time there was a Holy Ghost to receive. This could be most likely one of the many reasons and problems why many believers today are incomplete and without the gift of the Holy Ghost after they believe. They did not hear enough INFORMATION about it from the other believers or established churches. The job of the local churches are basically to equipped, instructed, and educated the believer after he or she believes the gospel about the Holy Ghost.

Now, I personally believe there are some believers that have believe the gospel and were baptize in water inside the local churches, and they have listen to the divine biblical messages from the preacher out of the pulpit on the Holy Ghost. But, they have not really heard or understood what the preacher or teacher was really saying. Jesus stated throughout the book of Revelation, "He that has an ear, let him (or her) <u>hear</u> what the Spirit of Truth says unto the church". A good example of listening but not hearing is John's disciples in Ephesus in Acts ch.19 verse 4. For they followed John the Baptist to the Jordan River, and they walked with John and they talked to John, but how is it they (the followers of John) did not clearly understand John. Surely, they were not paying close attention to what he was really saying. They were listening to John but not <u>hearing</u> the Baptist preacher.

For once again, John himself declared publicly to everyone including his disciples or followers in the book of Matthew ch.3 verse 11 to look to the one that comes after him, Jesus the Christ (the Anointed One) to receive the baptism of the Holy Ghost. Thanks be to God, the apostle Paul reminded the twelve disciples of John to believe on Jesus in Acts ch.19 verse 4, for after they <u>heard</u> and were reminded of what John the Baptist said, they were baptized in the name of the Lord Jesus, and received the Holy Ghost. After, the apostle Paul had laid his hands on them according to verse 6. This is another way the bible shows us on how to receive God's gift of the Holy Ghost by the laying of hands on them.

Most people do not like to be touch by other people especially by people who are complete strangers. The Holy Ghost is a necessity to the believer once he or she believes for without it, he or she will be a powerless and incomplete believer. There are some powerless, incomplete Christian believers in the world today, but I have good news for you, and it is you can become a powerful, and complete Christian full of the Holy Ghost power.

Some believers have received the power of the Holy Ghost by the laying of hands on them by other filled Holy Ghost believers, so ask God the Supreme Creator for it and wait patiently for it. Another word for wait is to <u>tarry,</u> according to 2 Samuel ch.15 verse 28.

Finally, there is one last traditional way of receiving the Holy Ghost that I know of according to scriptures and that is located in the book of Luke ch.24 verse 49, when Jesus told his disciples to go tarry (wait) in Jerusalem, and he will send the promise of the Father (the Holy Ghost) to them and then they will be empower from on High. The disciples prayed and waited patiently for two weeks or 10 days after the 40th day ascension of Jesus, which combined a total of 50 days after the Passover called Pentecost, until the Holy Ghost finally came upon them in the book of Acts ch.2 verse one. I know most people do not like waiting and at times I am very guilty of this process.

However, I do know from personal experience if you wait patiently for the Holy Ghost it is worth the wait. While you are waiting for the eternal promise of the Holy Spirit to come, for the Holy Ghost is Spirit, please remember the most important element or thing to do while you wait is to pray. Jesus stated in Luke ch.18 verse 1 that "Men should always pray, and not to faint" (or lose heart).

In addition, the book of Acts ch.1 verse 14 states the disciples continued with one accord in prayer (asking) and supplication (requesting) being made known unto God. The disciples were praying first for the Holy Ghost and waiting patiently second for the gift's arrival. I am not declaring 10 or 50 days from now a believer after accepting the Lord Jesus as Savior and being baptized in natural water will receive the Holy Ghost like the disciples did, for only God himself can make that proclamation.

However, God will give you the Gift when he is ready for you to have it, but your position to receive it is to pray and wait with earnest expectations "until the spirit be poured upon (you) from on high" Isaiah ch.32 verse 15. As you have already read previously there are several different ways on how God gave and still gives the Holy Ghost to his Christian believers. My spiritual mentor the late Elder Leroy Trout received the Holy Ghost while praying and waiting at his home inside his bedroom. My wife and I received the gift of the Holy Ghost at church while praying and waiting. The apostle Paul received the Holy Ghost at the house of Judas through the laying on of hands of Ananias in the book of Acts ch.9 verse 17. You might receive it right now while reading the spiritual content written inside the very pages of this book.

The ways of receiving the gift of the Holy Ghost are listed throughout the bible, but the places where you can receive the Gift are numerous. At home while praying in the bedroom, in church in front of the altar, in the car (motionless) while listening to music from a gospel CD or radio station, praying with another believer on the telephone. But, however and wherever you receive the gift please remember these six important principles;

1.) The Lord's will is for every believer to be filled with the Holy Spirit (Ephesians ch.5 v 17-18) (Joel ch.2 v 28-29).

2.) After the gift comes, you the believer has tremendous divine power.

3.) Don't abuse or misuse the powerful gift once you have received it.

4.) Don't ever blaspheme the Holy Ghost (Read Mark ch.3 verse 29).

5.) The evidence of the gift of the Holy Spirit is speaking with new tongues, and tongues are a sign of the gift as well as considered a sacred heavenly language between God and you. (Read 1st Corinthians ch.14 verse 2 & Romans ch.8 verse 26).

6.) The gift is not for your selfish needs, but it is to be used and operated in and for the building of God's kingdom.

Some people as well as some Christians believe the Holy Ghost was only available to the disciples back then in the days of and after Pentecost. However, in the book of Hebrews ch.13 verse 8 states that Jesus is the same yesterday, and today, and forever". This same Jesus is still giving and filling his followers with the

Holy Ghost. Why is Jesus still giving the gift of the Holy Spirit to his children that believe on him?

To not only to equipped them for a certain task, but to give them power to overcome the world, their flesh (old sinful nature), and the devil. Also, to become an effective, productive witness in his kingdom for him and to the whole world (Read Isaiah ch.43 verse 10 & Acts ch.1 verse 8).

CHAPTER TWO

§ ᙇ

"None Should Perish"

Before I start this second chapter about what is God the Father's will, I must state first and foremost that it is not God's will that any little child or children should perish. For the book of Matthew ch.18 verse 14 states, "Even so it is not the will of your Father which is in heaven that one of these little ones should perish." It is also not God's will that any adult human being should perish, but that all humans: Whites, Blacks, Hispanics, Asians, Native Indians, Jews, and Gentiles alike should come to repentance according to 2 Peter ch.3 verse 9. This scripture applies to everyone in the human race including the wicked, for God himself declared in the book of Ezekiel ch.18 verse 23, "Have I any pleasure at all that the wicked (person) should die?" After Almighty God asked the question in verse 23, he then gives us the answer to the question in verse 32" For I have no pleasure in the death of him (the wicked person) that die." The remedy for the wicked person as well as all humans is to repent and turn from all of their transgressions, so iniquity will not be their ruin according to verse 30.

Even if the Chancellor Adolf Hitler of Germany repented of all of his horrific sins before he died, God in his Supreme grace and infinite mercies would have forgave him. For the book of Romans ch.5 verse 20 states, "Where sin abounded, grace abound much more." Sin is destructive by nature and grows very rapidly at ongoing speed like a snowball traveling down a snowy hilltop mountain accumulating more snow and expanding larger in size. Destroying everything in its pathway causing a lot of damage, and eventually once the hill comes to an abrupt end, upon sudden impact, the snowball completely destroys itself. I want to use this picture of winter as an illustration for the apostle Paul's statement about grace abounding much more, and it is sin represents the snowball and grace represents the wintry mountain by which the growing snowball travels downward upon.

Also, sin is very appalling in itself in the sight of God. If people would look at sin through God eyes, they would see the repulsiveness of it. A good example on how sin looks to God is to look at his only begotten son Jesus before he was actually crucified by the Roman soldiers after he was beaten, bruised, and smitten alive on the whipping post. This is not a pretty picture to look upon like the one Leonardo da Vinci painted as the Lord's Last Supper in (1498).

After the Roman soldiers finished beating and spitting upon our Canaan King, Jesus himself looked like a hideous sea monster. Drench in his own sweat, blood, and tears from the onlookers of Jewish women along with Roman saliva, he continued to despise the shame for the joy of our salvation that was set before him enduring the cross. Now Jesus is sitting down at the right hand (a place of great supreme authority) of the throne of God, according to the book of Hebrews ch.12 verse two.

This gives people a complete insight, and a closer glimpse as well as a descriptive picture on how sin looks in the sight of God. For according to scripture Jesus himself not only looked like sin, but became the very essence of sin once, and for all of us (the whole entire human race) (2 Corinthians ch.5 verse 21). Jesus was the perfect sacrificial lamb and scapegoat, for the sins of the human world that shed his innocent blood when the Roman soldier pierced him in his precious side.

In Roman times, history proved many criminals were sentence to death punishable by crucifixion; however, even though many were crucified only one was pierced in the side. After the Roman soldier pierced Jesus in his side with a spear, according to John ch.19 verse 34. The pericardium sac that surrounded the heart plus the heart itself of Jesus which contained the blood (the life source of Divinity and humanity) and water was puncture, along with the blood came flowing and gushing out of him spilling onto the natural ground of mother earth.

I believe earth has some characteristics of a woman and that is why she is properly address as mother earth for why else would Jesus say in the book of Mark ch.4 verse 28, "The earth bring forth fruit of herself." Notice the word herself that God's son Jesus stated about the big blue planet, he created referring to earth as the female gender, and when his blood came flowing out of him upon her (earth) at the hillside of Golgotha. I believe mother earth was so shell shock by the outcome and shook herself with disbelief within as the bible mentions in the book of Matthew ch.27 verse 51 that "The earth did quake and the rocks rent."

For example, when someone is physically hurt or even murder in front of a man or woman, and the blood from the innocent victim comes gushing out. The looking bystander would become hysterical, traumatize, and emotionally disturbed in their nature and begin to shake with disbelief within. The blood of Jesus is so sacred, holy, and pure that when it felled on mother earth. I believe because of its purification, earth was stained and saturated by it, for she purified herself by screaming so loudly that it awoke the dead bodies of the saints that were sleeping in the graveyards and caused the graves to open their mouths wide. So, the saints could appear after Christ resurrected to the many people located in the holy city of Jerusalem (Matthew ch.27 verses 52 & 53).

At the beloved cross, a cruel Roman criminal instrument of torture and death where seeming defeat is turn into a great victory. Jesus declared in the book of John ch.12 verses 31 & 32, "Now shall (or will) the prince (the devil) of this world be cast out, and I, if I (Jesus) be lifted up (by crucifixion of the cross) from the earth, (the cross) will draw (bring) all men unto me." This is where salvation begins and the judgment of God's wrath ends for the Christian believer.

A beautiful illustration of this victory is found in the book of Judges Ch.14 verse 5 when Samson the strongest physical man in the Old Testament as well as Israel's deliver from the hands of their enemy, which were the Philistines, came in conflict with a young lion. After the Spirit of God came upon Samson, he strangled and defeated the young (arrogant and prideful) lion without any sharp instruments in his hands. For according to verse number 8, after Samson defeated the lion, a little while later he returned for his beloved bribe to be, and he discovered inside the dead carcass of the lion a swarm of bees and honey. Samson scooped the honey out of the carcass with his bare hands in spite of all the bee stings and ate some and offered the remaining to his parents, and they ate it as well.

I believe Samson is an Old Testament clone or shadow type of the great deliver of humanity Jesus the Christ. Jesus was the strongest spiritual man alive in the New Testament and delivered humanity from their enemy of sin and the roaring young lion (the devil –Read Psalm 91 verse 13) at the cross of Cavalry. Jesus defeated prideful Satan without any problems or weapons in his hands, for the exception of sharp nails piercing both of his hands and feet.

Now that the Lord Jesus conquered Satan, the young and old roaring lion, plus the swarm of bees of principalities and powers with their harmful and hurtful bee stings. All of the Christian believers can find honey (the sweet taste of victory) in the dead carcass plus total satisfaction and abundant life as well as strength for themselves and for all their family members and friends.

Currently, the cross is a symbol of great love and exchange as well as God's only key to ultimate victory. The believers wait with faith to see Jesus return one day for his chosen bribe (the church), so she can go on her eternal honeymoon (the rapture) with him as they meet in the air and live happily together forever.

I often wonder why God Almighty chose to use this certain instrument the cross as a way to eliminate sin and open the door for redemption to humanity until one day I looked very carefully at a picture of a cross and slightly tilted the picture and notice a remarkable resemblance. The cross tilted looked like and was similar to the letter X in the English alphabet. This signifies that God only used this symbol to mark out our many sins from the earth, for the letter X in mathematics represents the unknown.

If unbelievers decide and choose to repent of their sins, and accept the forgiveness of Jesus as well as making him Lord and Savior of their lives. Then their personal sins become unknown to God, for God said I will remember their sins no more in the book of Jeremiah ch.31 v 34.

Many people that read this book should learn from the lesson that the Roman Emperor Saint Constantine learned. After he had a dream of himself looking up at the night sky at the stars and saw the words in Greek saying "Conquer in this sign," for the stars gather themselves into a small (t) formation of a cross.

God stated in Psalms 147 verse 4 that he calls all the stars by their names, so the stars that formed themselves together in the sign of the cross in Constantine's dream was God's doing. Once most of us have learned to conquer life in the sign of the cross then many of us will become more than conquerors (two of the greatest military conquerors of all times in my opinion was Hannibal and Alexander the Great) through Jesus that loves us, according to the book of Romans Ch. 8 verse 37.

The love of God is longsuffering toward humanity so none of us should perish and a good analogy of this is located in the Old Testament scriptures. In the book of 2 Samuel Ch. 16 verse 11, "David said to Aisha and to all his servants, Behold, my son which came forth of my bowels seek my life." David was King over Israel at this particular time in biblical history and his own son Absalom was successor to the throne. Instead of waiting patiently to be the next heir, through his impatience, he wanted to overthrow his father's legendary reign by force and begin his own. Even though Absalom was a royal spoiled brat, born from the loins and bowels of a royal King and into a royal family, he became on his own accord a prince of deceit and rebellion.

This is how the wicked person and rebellious Christian is seen in the sight of God except for God is still reigning King over the entire Universe whereas David was (past tense) King over Israel. Absalom represents the wicked person as well as the rebellious Christian throughout the entire text for as he was created from the bowels of his father David, the wicked person and rebellious Christian are created from and in the likeness and image of their Father God. However, instead of trying to take God the Father's eternal life and power from him, they overthrow God's holy commandments through disobedience and end their own spiritual life for eternity.

According to the Old Testament, the book of Malachi ch.1 verse 14 states that "God is a great King" over the entire Universe, and he created the wicked person as well as the rebellious Christian to not live independently of him, but to live and walk humbly before him as an obedient prince in this world.

A good example of this type of humility lifestyle is mention in 2 Samuel Ch. 14 verse 33, "and (Absalom) bowed himself on his face to the ground before the King ;(David) and the King kissed Absalom. Notice what occurred immediately after Absalom (the prince) humble himself before his earthly father King David.

His father King David kissed him and likewise will God do himself if the wicked person or rebellious Christian will humble themselves in prayer daily before the King of Kings. For the Bible declares in the book of 2 Chronicles ch.7 verse 14, "If my people, which are called by my name, shall humble themselves and pray, and seek my face and turn (means to repent) from their wicked ways; then will I (God) hear from heaven (their prayers) and will forgive their sin, and will heal their land."

The turning from wicked ways and to God is known as repentance and if the wicked person or rebellious Christian does not turn from their wicked ways and continue in their sinful wickedness then ultimately their fate will be the same as Absalom's fate in 2 Samuel ch.18 verses 8, 9, & 14. "For the battle was there scattered over the face of all the country: and the wood (forest) devoured more people that day than the sword devoured." Absalom met the servants of David and Absalom rode upon a mule and the mule went under the thick boughs of a great oak, and his head (hair) caught hold of the oak, and he was taken up between the heaven and the earth; and the mule that was under him went away." Then said Joab, I may not (wait or) tarry thus with thee, and he took three darts (spears) in his hand, and thrust them through the heart of Absalom while he was alive in the midst of the oak (tree forest)."

This was a very tragic ending for Absalom the prince of Israel and will also be a bitter ending for the wicked person as well as the rebellious Christian if they do not repent of their wicked ways, except for a great oak tree in the forest crabbing and entrapping them by their hair, which represents human intelligence. The forest or wilderness of life will eventually, powerfully overtake them and hold them hostage against their own will until sudden death arrives, and sends something or someone like (Joab) to execute them as they are caught helplessly between the bottom of hell and on the middle ground of earth and the balconies of heaven.

In addition, the most important lesson about the story of Absalom while he was alive he yet stated about himself in 2 Samuel ch.14 the ending of verse 32 that "if there be any iniquity in me, let him (King David his father) kill me". I can truly state to the wicked person and rebellious Christian that if their heart is filled with the iniquity of darkness, he or she will harmfully kill their own spiritual soul in the second death according to the book of Revelation ch.21 verse 8.

In his book "Life Overflowing" written by Bishop T.D. Jakes, he gave a simple analogy about light and darkness. Jakes asked a question in his book if darkness could enter into a well- lighted room and the answer was and always will be no. The only way darkness could enter into a well- lighted room is if someone or something turns off the lights by the light switch or if the lights are automatically going off by a timer or an electrical storm causes a complete blackout or power failure. The bible declares in 1st John ch.1 verse 5 that "God is light, and in him is <u>no darkness</u> at all," so a heart filled with the darkness of iniquity cannot enter or live in heaven in fellowship with "the Father of lights"(James ch.1 verse 17) for eternity.

The results of disobedience and rebellion is found in 2 Samuel ch.14 verse 24, when King David said "Let him (Absalom) turn to his <u>own house</u>, (the place of dwelling) and let him not see my face," so Absalom returned to his own house and saw not the King's face." The wicked person and rebellious Christian will not see the face of God if they continue in their wickedness, for only the pure in heart will see God according to Matthew ch.5 verse eight.

They (the wicked person and rebellious Christian) will return to their own house (the place of dwelling forever) in the eternal lake of fire. Hell and destruction was never intended for human souls, but hell and the destruction of the lake of fire was solely for the purpose of the devil and the one third of demons (Revelation ch.12 verse 4) that felled from heaven with him. God loves and cares for the souls of men for God said "All souls are mine," in the book of Ezekiel ch.18 verse four. God is deeply concerned for the human souls and their safety.

Even though the story of Absalom ends as a tragic story ending in his physical death, I noticed in 2 Samuel ch.18 verses 29 & 32 how King David inquired twice about his own son's safety. "And the king said, Is the young man Absalom safe?" in verse 29, and the king said unto Cushi is the young man Absalom safe in verse 32. I also want to say twice that God is deeply concerned about his own created souls and their safety as well.

Also, I would like to emphasize great emphasis to the response of King David after he receives the terrible news of the death of his very own son in 2 Samuel ch.18 verse 33. "And the king was much moved, and went up to the chamber over the gate, and wept: and as he went, he said, O my son Absalom, my son Absalom! Would God I had died for thee (you), O Absalom, my son, my son!"

The king of Israel was deeply moved and overcome with the emotion of grief which caused him to burst into many tears. I believe God the Father is moved with the emotion of grief and suffers sorrow over his very own created human souls that lives in rebellion against him and are made in his likeness and image. For the main and sole purpose for the original creation of all human being souls are specifically created to wear an incorruptible crown of glory and honor like a royal diadem on the head of a royal prince instead of wearing a rebellious corruptible crown of disloyalty and dishonor.

There are five eternal crowns listed below with the place of scripture that the Royal King of the Universe wants to give to them that love him and are subject to the rules and laws of his holy Royal Kingdom.

1.) An Incorruptible Crown or the Everlasting Crown – (1st Corinthians ch.9 verse 25)

2.) The Crown of Rejoicing also named the Soul Winner's Crown – (1st Thessalonians ch.2 verse 19)

3.) The Crown of Life - (James ch.1 verse 12)

4.) A Crown of Righteousness – (2 Timothy ch.4 verse 8)

5.) A Crown of Glory – (1st Peter ch.5 verse 4)

"The Aftermath of the Afterlife"

The Bible states that there is life after death when a person dies and death is not the final end, but only the beginning and this is the main reason why chapter three was given its title "The Aftermath of the Afterlife." For in the book of Mark ch.12 verse 23, a religious sect called the Sadducees, which say and believe that there is no resurrection, asked Jesus about a certain woman who was married seven times with no children. They asked "Whose wife will she be in the resurrection?" Jesus responded in verse 25 by saying when (and not if) they (the dead people) shall rise from the dead, they neither marry nor are given in marriage, but are as the angels which are in heaven."

After the physical aftermath of death, man or woman will no longer be governed by the physical laws of nature and marriage, but he or she will have an immortal body nature like the angels in a spirit world in the spiritual afterlife. Jesus also stated in verse 27 that God is not the God of the dead (people or saints), but the God of the living. Abraham, Isaac, and Jacob had long been dead by the time God spoke this to Moses, and God still talked about them as if they were yet alive, so the only possible explanation is they were still alive and that there is life after death.

Another incident in the scriptures whereas deceased saints or prophets were seen alive together with Jesus himself is found in the book of Luke ch.9 verse 30, when "Moses and Elijah appeared and began talking with Jesus." Moses and Elijah were the two greatest prophets in the Old Testament. Moses represented the law, which was the old covenant, because he wrote the Pentateuch. Elijah represented the prophets who foretold the coming of the Messiah. Moses and Elijah's presence with Jesus confirmed Jesus messianic mission to fulfill God's law and the words of God's prophets.

Also, these godly men discussed with Jesus his departure or exodus to accomplish at Jerusalem. Jesus was about to make a great transition from having an existence on earth in the flesh to having an existence again in heaven in the spirit. Jerusalem was the starting point of this exodus because Jerusalem was the place of his death and resurrection. Jesus was the first fruit of the resurrection that ascended into heaven and led the exit or exodus of captives (slaves to sin) out of captivity (bondage to death) into the promise land of heaven that flows with milk and honey.

Although Jesus experience death by crucifixion, Elijah did not actually experience death with his physical body. For he received a private escort by a chariot of fire and horses of fire to be taken up by a whirlwind into heaven that was specifically sent by God after he crossed the Jordan river (2 Kings Ch.2 verse 11).

On the other hand, Moses who was called Israel's greatest prophet as a national leader and powerful orator. Seeing as, he was the only person that ever spoke with God face to face

(Exodus ch.33 verse 11), and did died physically in the land of Moab when he was one hundred and twenty years old (Deuteronomy ch.34 verses 5-7). The ascended life into heaven of Elijah and the experience of the natural physical death of Moses were Biblical patterns for Jesus to follow after his life ended physically at the cross. Jesus was quicken from the dead and ascended into heaven for eternity.

After his physical mission on earth and his spiritual ascension into heaven was completed, Jesus sat down at the right hand of the throne of God according to the book of Hebrews ch.12 verse two. Jesus sitting down at the right hand of the throne of God is a place of position and authority.

For the mother of James and John, the sons of Zebedee asked Jesus if they could sit down by him on his right and left hand side when they arrived in heaven, but Jesus told them in the book of Matthew ch.20 verse 23 that it was not his right to give to say who will sit on the thrones next to his of the top positions of leadership in heaven because they are decided by God the Father alone.

However, Jesus extends the personal invitation to all of us to come join in and sit down in the kingdom of heaven with him and Abraham, Isaac, and Jacob (Matthew ch.8 verse 11). I personally believe there are many reserved seats in heaven for Jesus said that many will come from the east, west, south, and north to fill them.

There is an old saying that the proof is in the pudding, and I want to add to it by saying the pudding is the delicious gospel of Jesus Christ. The Biblical scriptures proves that there is life after death, and the place where Jesus sits is a place of great position and supreme authority like a federal chief judge sitting on the bench inside the U.S. Supreme courthouse.

In heaven, Jesus is the eternal and sovereign judge of all human beings, for the book of 2 Timothy ch.4 verse one declares that "The Lord Jesus Christ shall judge the quick (or living) and the dead at his appearing and his Kingdom." In order to be appointed the Eternal Judge of humanity the chief judge himself must be entirely worthy and his judgment factual, just, and true. The judgment of Jesus Christ is not only just, according to the book of John ch.5 verse 30, but all judgment has been committed to him because God the Father judges no man according to John ch.5 verse 22.

For in the book of Hebrews ch.9 verse 27 states," That it is appointed unto men to die, but after death then comes the judgment." In actuality, Jesus himself does not judge the one that rejects him or his message, but the word that he spoken does according to the book of John ch.12 verse 48. Before a person stands before God's son to be judge by the word of God for the crime of their many sins, if he or she repents and confess those crimes and asked for total forgiveness plus accepted Jesus as Lord and Savior while he or she were still alive on earth then the guilt and penalty of those sinful crimes were already judge and forgiven. This means the person is declared freedom and is totally innocent of all charges against him or her and he or she cannot be tried twice for the same crime when standing before the judgment seat of Christ after death. The technical term for this procedure in the earth's court of law is called double jeopardy. A person cannot be tried or judge twice for the same crime or crimes.

The book of Romans ch.8 verse one states, "There is therefore now no condemnation to them which are in Christ Jesus, who walk not after the flesh, but after the spirit." Notice here what the Apostle Paul is saying to the church in Rome, for there is an old saying "When you are in Rome, do as the Romans do", however; Paul was advising the Christians located in Rome to do the exact opposite, for the Romans walked and ran after their flesh and try to fulfill its many lustful desires. Paul informed the Christians to live the rest of their natural life walking in the Holy Spirit of a new man, for the flesh was very weak rapidly aging and dying like an old man.

The old man is not only known as the flesh, but the old sinful nature as well, and the new man is considered the new creature or the newness of life in Christ as well as the inner Spirit man. The old man (the flesh) is in a constant battle with the new man (the inner Spirit) and the outcome of victory in the war is decided upon which one is fed the most. When the old man vs. the new man, the word verses caught in between the middle of the two is represented as the human soul. The soul itself decides which man old or new will win the entire war.

A joke was told to me once that a gigantic Robot had two dogs living on the inside of him. A white one and a black one and they fought constantly against each other every day all the time, so I asked the guy telling me this corny joke, which dog won the fight. His response was the one that the robot fed the most. After hearing this joke, I finally understood how to defeat the old man within myself through starvation and feeding the new man by studying, praying, and doing God's word on a daily basis.

Another example of the old man vs. the new man is located in the book of Luke ch.5 verses 37 -38 when Jesus stated, "No man put new wine into old bottles, else the new wine will burst the bottles and spilled and the old bottles shall perish or be ruined, but new wine must be put into new bottles and both are preserved." In bible times, wine was not stored in glass bottles, but in wineskins which were made out of goatskin sewed together at the edges to form a watertight bag.

A goat in the Bible represented the old sinful nature of man. New wine had to be placed and stored inside new wineskin bottles, for new wine expanded as it aged plus fermented and produce gas stretching the wineskin.

An old wineskin bottle could not be used to store or carry new wine, because it had already been previously stretched to the fullest degree, and with no more possible room for stretching, it would eventually burst. The human heart of many people can be rough, tough, and rigid like an old wineskin bottle having no flexibility in their heart for growth and change of spiritual development nor accepting the new wine (lifestyle), which is the life changing truths of Jesus Christ. Also, the old sinful nature (the flesh) is like an old goat wineskin bottle for it does not accept, like, or love the new wine or life teachings of Jesus.

The new wine in the Bible is represented as a biblical representation of the Holy Spirit in the book of Acts ch.2 verse 13. Furthermore, the new wineskin bottle is the fleshy heart of a new man filled with the new wine of the Holy Spirit and is preserved to be sent out of God's glorious kingdom.

A good example of this is the bottles of Pepsi and Coke products being sent out throughout the entire world to mainstream consumers for drinking consumption. Each consumer decides their preferable taste of Pepsi or Coke, after the manufacturers has release and distributes their products. The manufacturing plant is the kingdom of God making disciples (bottles) of men filling them with the Holy Ghost (new wine), and releasing or sending them out to everyone and every generation.

The product (bottle of Pepsi or Coke) normally arrives at its final destination which is in the hands of men after being purchased at the nearest store location. Shortly after, the cap is usually removed from the bottle and tasted by the consumer. The disciples (which are bottles of men) follow this same pattern in a sense when they finally arrive, and meet unbelievers in their life's journey and introduce the good quality tasting news of the gospel to the unbelievers.

After the unbelievers decide to taste or try Jesus for themselves, shortly after, they will soon discover that Jesus is sweeter than honey from the honeycomb. For the Bible declares in Psalms 34 verse 8 "O taste and see (for yourself) that the Lord (Jesus) is good." Hopefully, all of the unbelieving hearts of the unbelievers are acceptable plus elastic, open and flexible, for adapting to change to the life changing teachings and truths of Jesus like a new wineskin bottle.

I want to share a wonderful secret and incredible truth to the filled Holy Ghost believers, which are infused inside with supernatural power, and that is don't ever forget to constantly stir up or shake up the gift laying on the inside of you which is similar to shaking up and down a bottle of Pepsi or Coke.

As the chemical acids and mixed natural chemicals in these products causes fizzing and possibly a pop explosion if the top is remove after being shaken. I caution but also urging the Christian saints that are filled with the Holy Ghost to spiritually shake up themselves daily, and release a spiritual explosion everyday by witnessing about Jesus as well as praying continually for a spiritual revival throughout all of our nations.

A pastor I once knew by the name of Elder Charles Towns who went home to be with the Lord once stated to me that he loved to drink black coffee without cream, but with a reasonable amount of sugar. He said if he did not stir up the coffee and the sugar combine with a plastic or metal spoon he could not taste the sweetness of the sugar, for the sugar he poured in remained dormant and tasteless until it was fully stirred by him.

It was then Pastor Towns receive a special word from the Holy Ghost, and perceived the revelation that in order for the Holy Ghost believers to taste the entire sweetness of the Holy Spirit in their own life's, they must first stir up the gift that was placed inside them according to 2 Timothy ch.1 verse six.

Before I close out chapter three, I want to discuss and explain about the unfruitful or unproductive servant in God's kingdom. According to the book of Mark ch.11 verse 12, Jesus curses a fruitless unproductive fig tree. Jesus and his disciples came from Bethany to the village of Bethphage. The village of Bethphage was in the same neighborhood as Bethany and got its name "house of figs" or better known as fig country.

Jesus was hungry and saw from a distance a fig tree full of large green leaves, but after examining the tree close up he discovered no fruit of any kind. Fig trees in Israel require three years from the time they were planted until the time they could bear any fruit. Each fig tree yielded a great amount of fruit twice a year.

However, before fig trees could produce large green leaves they produced small edible buds and the buds would drop off when the leaves fully developed. The figs normally grew with the leaves when the leaves filled out and became visibly apparent. The buds that dropped off the tree and the figs as well were eaten by peasants, and they both were considered a popular source of inexpensive food in Israel. In Jesus' day, a fruit tree without fruit was useless so he curse it, however his curse did not make the tree barren for it was already barren, but it did sealed the way the tree has always been.

The curse did more than condemn the tree to a barren life for it killed it completely. In other words, the curse of Jesus sealed the fate of the tree forever. This particular fig tree showed potential and promise of abundant fruit, but it produced none except large green glossy leaves.

The Pharisees and the Jewish religion in Jesus day was all show (green leaves) with no spiritual reality of fruit. Having a form of godliness, but denying the power thereof according to 2 Timothy ch.3 verse five. By cursing the fig tree, I believe Jesus was demonstrating his dissatisfaction and anger at a religious life without any substance of spiritual fruit.

The Bible states "Faith without works is dead," and faith produces doers which requires and involves action for without action faith is dead and dead faith is worse than no faith according to the King James Bible. Jesus wants us to be focus, faithful, and fruitful in his kingdom. The unfruitful, and unproductive servant in God's kingdom is like this barren fig tree which is fruitful in physical appearance only from a far distance with large green leaves, but spiritually naked without substance up close.

To all of the Christian believers, please remember what you are supposed to be doing here on earth. Moreover, not just accepting blessings like this fig tree which was soaking up all the time God's resources such as: the sun, the rain, along with his wonderful air, always living and being planted firmly in the deep soil of God's green grass on earth.

I believe all Christian believers are supposed to be doing on earth is living like a tree planted by the rivers of water that bring forth their fruit in their season (twice a year) and our leaf (or leaves) shall not wither (away), but whatsoever we (decide to) do shall prosper according to Psalm one verse three.

In closing, Jesus gave the great commission to all of us in the book of Matthew ch.28 verse 19, which is to go "Teach and preach the gospel to all nations and to every creature", furthermore; I ultimately believe this is what we are supposed to be doing as Christian individuals on earth. When the time comes for us individually to be examine closely by Jesus in the Aftermath of the Afterlife, he will not find us fruitless and unproductive in this life and curse us into hell's eternity forever.

CHAPTER FOUR

"Divinity's will vs. humanity's will"

W hat would happen if God himself was involved in a wrestling competition here on earth, not as a special guest referee, but as a contender or challenger against man? Who would win between God verses man or God's will vs. man's will? This might be a rhetorical question because everyone knows the answer is God.

However, in the book of Genesis ch.32 verse 24 there is a Biblical story about a man named Jacob who was involved in a wrestling match against God on earth. The name of Jacob means deceiver or manipulator, and Jacob lived up to the expectations of his own name when he deceived his father Isaac by disguising himself as his brother Esau, so he could steal his brother's blessing.

This wrestling match between God and Jacob was an all-night match. There were no time limits to this match, no angel referee's, and no disqualifications. It was a winner take all match, Divinity's will verses humanity's will. The holy match took place centered stage at a place called Peniel. It was the most anticipating match of the century.

The undefeated heavyweight champion of the universe verses a mere moral, but the only way this match could take place is God had to appear to Jacob in a physical human form. This is called a theophany where God came in the physical form of a man to wrestle against Jacob. For Jacob had at least one or two victories underneath his belt for the NIV Bible translation states in Genesis ch.32 verse 28, "You (Jacob) have struggled with both God and <u>men</u> and have won".

Whenever I read this story about God verses Jacob in a wrestling match, I noticed during the match God showed Jacob that he could easily physically disable him at any time by one touch to his hip which caused severe damage, plus knocked it out of joint at the socket. The thigh muscle which is one of the strongest muscles in the body was severely damage by God and by touching his hip, God caused Jacob to be in a lot of physical pain.

On the other hand, his endurance through the pain kept him persistent, for when God said in verse 26, "Let me go, for the day break" (or the sun is rising), Jacob responded by saying, "I will not let thee (you) go, except thou (you) bless me." God could had easily broken free from Jacob's grasp, but I believe God wanted to stay and bless Jacob just like he wants to bless all of his children. However, for Jacob's persistent, I believe God let Jacob win the wrestling match, so he could bless him and reward him for his persistent.

For example, I have two sons and one daughter, and when I wrestle against my two sons, who are the younger ages of 14 and 13 plus a lot smaller than me, most of the time I let them get the better of me, and sometimes I even let them win to build their confidence. I could easily dominate all of the wrestling matches and win every time and disable my two sons anytime because of my physical size, strength, and weight.

However, as a loving earthy father I not only enjoyed the physical contact with them and the wrestling activity itself, but I also enjoyed seeing their persistence to win against me. I believe God is a heavenly, loving father who let his son Jacob pin and hold him, so he could bless him and changed his name from Jacob, the ambitious deceiver to the honest prince of Israel, the father of the twelve tribes and one who struggle with God and overcame. The new name that Jacob received was a symbol of how God had changed his life and his character identity for Jacob's true identity came from eternity.

Dr. Martin Luther King Jr. once stated "Intelligence plus character (of integrity) that is the goal of (or that equals) true education." Jacob was intelligent enough to know that God could change his character of deceiving, tricking, and lying to a character of integrity in one all night wrestling match, which he learned truth through his experience, plus a valuable lesson of spiritual education to help him succeed in life, and to help those that believe also receive the gospel in the distant future.

This same spiritual lesson applies to all Christian believers, and Jacob is a spiritual role model for all of us to follow, "For we wrestle not against flesh and blood, but against principalities, against powers, against the rulers of the darkness of this world, against spiritual wickedness in high places" according to Ephesians ch.6 verse 12. The life of Jacob has taught me that our wrestling matches do not take place on earth, but in the spirit realm with persistent prayer to God to overcome many dark spiritual opponents.

Jacob's life has also taught me that no matter how long it takes in prayer, all day or all night, all week, all month, or all year to stay consistent and persistent with prayer through my struggles of pain in life, and God will bless me

In closing, all Christian believers and non-believers alike must realize whenever Divinity's will vs. humanity's will in a competed match that God's will always prevails. During the match, God showed us with Jacob at any time, he has the supernatural ability to overpower man's will unless man totally surrenders his will in exchange for God's will then will man see a full transformation of his personal life and experience the abundant life of Jesus Christ.

The abundant life has nothing to do with an abundance of material possession, financial prosperity or guarantee popular success in ministry or a fabulous million dollar career, but the abundant life of Christ is <u>the abundance of good works</u> for his kingdom.

CHAPTER FIVE

"Heaven Bound"

There is a book out entitled "I Hope They Serve Beer in Hell" written by Tucker Max and the title of this book sounds very dangerous and deceptive.

I have not personally read this book, for the title alone is quite disturbing, plus in the book of Luke ch.16 verse 24 proves to whoever reads it that there will be no liquid beverages given or served in hell.

However, Jesus stated in the book of Matthew ch.26 verse 29 that the fruit of the vine (or wine) will be served in heaven. A messianic banquet is given in honor of our Lord and Savior Jesus Christ as well as everyone on this earth is given freely an invitation to eat and drink at his royal table inside his heavenly kingdom according to Luke ch.22 verse 30.

The spiritual reality of this universal invitation is not everyone will accept God's wonderful offer to his heavenly banquet and go to heaven, for the exception of those that are Heaven bound. Did you know the only ones that are going to heaven are the ones who do God's will? Why else would Jesus say in the book of Matthew ch.7 verse 21, "Not everyone that says unto me (Jesus) Lord, Lord, shall enter into the kingdom of heaven, but he(or she) <u>that do the will of my father</u> which is in heaven."

The Holy Spirit brought this to my attention a long time ago when I was reading this verse of scripture at my mother's kitchen table right after I was born again, and filled with the Holy Ghost, the special emphasizes on doing the will of God the Father. I remember asking the Holy Spirit plainly what is the will of God the Father, and I thought to myself how can I do his will if I do not even know what his will is? The Holy Spirit kept silent right after he told me to continue reading the Bible and I would soon discover what the will of God the Father was and still is. I continued to read the bible at my mom's kitchen table full of expectancy, joy, and excitement.

As I continued to read the book of Matthew, five chapters later I came across another verse of scripture in Matthew ch.12 verse 50 where Jesus declared "For whosoever shall do the will of my Father which is in heaven, the same is my brother, sister, and mother."

Once again I was amazed at the hidden message of truth found in the scripture for "whosoever <u>shall do the will of God the Father</u> the same is my brother, sister, and mother." Jesus had earthly natural siblings after he was born, but this statement by him declares how to become heavenly spiritual relatives. The book of Matthew and Mark both gave an accurate account of this same statement by Jesus in Mark ch.3 verse 35.

<u>The will of my Father</u> kept magnifying itself on the pages of the bible in giant bold print and was highlighted as if God himself was shining a beam of light from heaven to pay close special attention to it. The words of the text not only engulfed me, but

entreated me even more to find out what was the will of God for me and my life. How was I to find out and discover God the Father's will?

There was no loud audible voice speaking to me through a flaming burning bush like in the days of Moses in the book of Exodus chapter three. On the other hand, like in the book of 1st Kings ch.19, there was the Holy Spirit whispering in my ear in a still small voice reminding me of the words of Jesus what I previously read in the book of Matthew ch.7 verses 7- 8. "Ask, and it shall be given you; seek, and you shall find; knock, and it shall be opened unto you." For everyone that asks receive; and he that seeks finds, and to him that knock it shall be open."

To discover God's will, I not only had to asked God in faith alone to show me his will, but I had to place my faith in action by searching and reading the scriptures to find out what his will was. I knock on heaven's door through prayer and asked God to reveal to me what was hidden in these verses of scriptures which was the mystery of his will. I wanted a quick and simply but powerful response.

To make a long story short, I read all of the three gospels Matthew, Mark, and Luke, and I still did not know or come closer to discovering what God's divine will was. I went to my bedroom exhausted from reading the bible and said my evening prayers to God in spite of my discouragement, and as I arose off of my knees to get into my waterbed, I heard the Holy Spirit tell me to keep reading, for I was real close. Of course, this was encouraging statements from God which I really did not want to hear at that time, because of my impatience, for I wanted a quick response or answer, not something drawn out and engaging in a lifetime journey.

My mind was finally made up to go and explore God's word of wisdom and knowledge even if it took a life's journey in doing so, for no matter how long it took to discover God's will I was determine within myself to find out what his divine will was for my natural earthy life. The question remained how can I be Heaven Bound for glory not knowing the will of God the Father for my own personal life? Surely, I knew Almighty God would not hold me personally responsible for something I did not know.

Even though, I studied most of the New Testament and all of the Old Testament, I knew I was getting even closer to finding an exact answer to knowing the will of God the Father. For a while, I still continue reading without knowing, and then I stumbled across another great clue or vital piece of the mysterious puzzle that was found in the book of St. John ch.9 verse 31.

When a blind man testify about Jesus restoring his sight back to him, for he also publicly declared to the Pharisees "Now we know that God hear not sinners; but if any man be a worshipper of God and do his will, him he hears."

This was a remarkable statement coming from a blind man who once was blind and now could see the face of the religious leaders who could naturally see, but was spiritually blind. The stone faces of the Pharisees who practice hypocrisy stared long and hard at the blind man as he spoke and spiritually educated the piteous crowd of tough listeners.

They were so tough on the blind man that in verse 34 they answered and said unto him "Thou (you) was altogether born in sins, and do thou (you) teach us and they cast him out." What a comment by the Pharisees to make as if they were not born in sin and shaped in iniquity for the bible declared in the book of Romans ch.3 verse 23. "For all have sinned and come short of the glory of God" and all people were conceived in sin by their mothers according to King David in Psalms ch.51 verse five.

The Pharisees were not even trying to listen to or understand what the blind man was actually saying, but I know I did. There the words were staring at me once again in my face if any man be a worshipper of God and <u>do his will</u>, God hears him. First, I had to find out what was God's definition of a worshipper before I could find out his will.

A worshipper from the definition of Jesus is found in John ch.4 verses 23- 24. "The hour come and now is, when the true worshippers shall worship the Father in spirit and in truth, for (God) the Father seek such to worship him. "God is Spirit, and they (the genuine worshippers) that worship him must worship him <u>in spirit</u> and <u>in truth</u> (or reality).

I realize after reading this in the Bible there could be no jokes or horse playing when it comes to worshipping God, for God is a (Holy) Spirit and I had to worship him in my spirit and in reality of truth in order to get in touch with him about his will. I did not want to be a hearer only of God's word and will like most people, but I wanted to be a doer of his word and will like the book of James describe in ch.1 verse 22, and in order to do so I started taking my walk with God more seriously.

I started praying three times a day like King David found in Psalm 55 verse 17, "Morning, noon, and in the evening time will I pray." I went to bed praying in the spirit or I should say aloud in the Holy Ghost. I started praying daily and fasting twice a week to get even closer to God even though fasting without praying basically disciplines and denies the flesh from eating or overeating.

Instead of eating natural food, I replaced it by reading and studying the Bible to receive spiritual food for the nourishment of my soul. Not only did I receive my spiritual vitamins and antioxidants on a daily basis, but the more I read my bible the more I discovered a lot of other wonderful things about God.

For example, I learned some of the colors in the Bible have significant meanings. The color red represented the blood of atonement and the color white represented purity and holiness. The color of silver is for redemption and the color gold is for God's glory or divinity. The color yellow represents celebration or joy while the color green represents growth and fruitfulness of a new life.

The color bronze or brass represents humanity or God's divine judgment, for Revelation 1:15 says "the feet of Jesus were like bronze or fine brass" which stands for "his judgmental activity of stamping down" according to Gundry's book "A Survey of the New Testament." The color black represents sin and death, plus the color purple represents kingship and the color blue represents grace.

The amazing grace of the color blue is found in the book of Exodus ch.24 verses 10-11, For "they (Israel's 74 leaders) saw the God of Israel, and there was under his feet as it were a paved work of a sapphire (deep blue color of a gem) stone and as it were the body of heaven in his clearness." Webster's seventh new collegiate dictionary defines sapphire as a variable color averaging a deep purplish blue.

The color purple represents royalty kingship (see Mark ch.15 verse 17) and the color red that is for the blood of atonement mixed together with the color blue for a deep purplish blue color that represents the deepness of God's heavenly grace. All of the colors work together for red and blue makes purple.

Now wonder why, God in the following verse of 11, in the same chapter did not lay his hand upon the nobles (or leaders) of the children of Israel, for of his deep amazing grace. By grace, he also allowed the 74 leaders to see him as well as drink and eat a meal in his presence plus allowed all of them to live so they could tell their children all about the event.

Colors are not the only thing I learned within the bible that have significant meanings, but also numbers for numbers are the secret code of God's word. I'm not talking about the book of Numbers located in the Old Testament, however; I am referring to the numerical numbers of the Bible.

For instance, the number one in the Bible stands for strength and unity or unification. The number two in the Bible means separation for God made the firmament in Genesis ch.1 verses 7-8, and "divided (or separated) the waters which were under the firmament from the waters which were above the firmament; and it was so, and God called the firmament Heaven and the evening and the morning were the second day." The second day of creation is when God created the sky and the waters were separated.

Also, Jesus stated in the book of Matthew ch.19 verse 5 that a man will leave his father also mother and shall cleave to his wife, and they twain (or two will no longer be separated as two separate bodies in the flesh), but shall be one flesh. I want to take this step even further with the separation of the human spirit from the natural body which is called death. Separate one from the other, which equals the number two, and it will result in natural death known to all Bible readers and believers as the first death. However, the book of Revelation ch.20 verses 14-15 speaks of a second death which God will ultimately separate the two types of people that live in this world for eternity, the Christian believers from the non-believers.

The number three in the Bible represents the fullness of the Godhead or the Trinity which is similar to a hard-boiled egg. Three different manifestations made of as one entire egg. The yellow yoke or core that is formed inside of the egg is the center piece which could easily represent God the Father.

The soft white layer that surrounds the yoke would represent the Word of God which is Jesus Christ the Son of God. The hard white outer shell of the egg that protects, shields, hovers or covers over the earth would represent the Holy Spirit and these three are one and bear record in heaven according to 1st John ch.5 verse seven.

For according to verse eight in First John chapter five, there are also three that bear witness in <u>the earth</u> and these three agree in one which is the Spirit, the water, and the blood. The number four in the Bible represents the creation of <u>the earth</u> or the identity of Jesus the Christ. The number four relates to creation of the earth, for the earth has four seasons of winter, spring, summer, and fall. As well as the four corners or primary directions located in the earth which is north, east, south, and west. Also, there are four witnesses of God on earth which are miracles, signs, wonders, and the gifts of the Holy Spirit.

As far as the identity of Jesus the Christ, the four gospels Matthew, Mark, Luke, and John all write about their own account of experience with him. The four horsemen of the apocalypse in the book of Revelation, and the four living creatures as well as the four wheels in the book of Ezekiel, all represents Jesus' identity. The three Hebrew boys plus Jesus walking around in the fiery furnace equals the number four in the book of Daniel ch.3 verse 25. Jesus came through the lineage of Judah who was Leah's fourth son in the book of Genesis ch.29 verse 35.

The number five in the Bible represents Grace (for example, the Pentateuch are the first five books of the Bible), and the exact same meaning as the color blue. Here on earth there is black supremacy and white supremacy segregated by the division supremacy of racism, but Almighty God has created the ultimate supremacy of all which is blue supremacy or Grace Supremacy. Because of the Grace Supremacy of God, many Christians including myself who want to do the will of God are Heaven Bound for glory.

One of the main and most important reasons on why the Holy Spirit led me to entitle chapter five "Heaven Bound" is for the only way all of us can become Heaven Bound is because of God's grace. For the Bible states in the book of Ephesians ch.2 verse 8, "For by grace are you saved through faith; and that (faith is) not of yourselves. It is the gift of God."

CHAPTER SIX

"Yes We Can!"

T he year of 2008 was a historical momentously year for Africans Americans when Barack Obama became the first black president of the United States of America. His African name of Barack means "to be bless" and he was blessed indeed. For his campaign slogan of "Yes we can!" was echoed and chanted by millions of Americans across the nations to demonstrate a cry for help or call for radical change in the philosophy of republican politics illustrated in the White House. This slogan not only united Americans in unity around the world but it helped Americans believe in and keep hope alive for a better change to create a better future for all Americans.

I personally always wanted to know and often wonder why the Democrats chose the humble animal of a donkey to represent their party as its symbol when the Republican Party selected a big strong powerful elephant to represent them. In my opinion, Jesus could had very easily been a Democrat for in the book of John ch.12 verse 14, he selected as a means of transportation to ride on the back of a lowly donkey into the great city of Jerusalem.

However, the only person that I can think of that comes to mind who decided to ride on the back of an elephant is Hannibal before he went to war. Jesus did not ride a horse or an elephant into Jerusalem, for it would have sent the wrong message that he was a man of war.

I truly believe in my heart that Jesus was an independent member of both parties, politically and religiously only endorsing God the Father's campaign trail of saving the lost by dying on the cross and filling born again believers with the Holy Ghost. Jesus was neither both republican or Democrat, Pharisee or Sadducee, Greek or Gentile, but he was born fully human as the Son of man as a Jew, and he is most importantly the Son of the living God.

I also believe if Jesus returned to the earth today he would remind the Republican Party that his word states in 1st Timothy ch.6 verses 17 thru 19, "Charge them that are rich in this world, that they be not high-minded, nor trust in uncertain riches, but in **the living God**, who gives us richly all things to enjoy." That they do well, that they be rich in **good works**, ready to distribute (or give), willing to communicate (and share). " Laying up (heavenly treasures) in store for themselves a good foundation against the time to come that they may lay hold (to or) on eternal life." Likewise, Jesus would remind them "Blessed is the man that considers the poor (people)" in Psalm 41 verse 1, and to heal the sick physically and afflicted mentally by reforming national healthcare.

To the Democratic Party, Jesus would remind them to never compromise with sin such as abortion, for children are a blessing from the Lord, plus God the Father in the book of Jeremiah ch.1 verse 5 declared "Before I formed you in the belly (of your mother), I knew you."

Both parties are guilty in God's eyes and both parties need his help to improve in these areas. "For God so loved the world (Republicans and Democrats, Jews & Gentiles, Blacks and Whites, Asians & Hispanics, Native Indians and people from India) that he gave his only begotten son (Jesus) that whoever believes in him should not perish, but have everlasting life" (John ch.3 verse 16).

This chapter is not at all about politics or political views to endorse any certain party, but it is about political animal symbolism, Republican capitalism, word slogan and number symbolism. The popular campaign slogan that was used by the Democratic Party of "Yes we can!" could also be in comparison to the book of Philippians ch.4 verse 13, when the apostle Paul wrote in his epistle letter to the Philippians church "I can do all things through Christ which strengthens me".

In other words, the apostle Paul was saying "(<u>Yes</u>) I can do all things through Christ which strengthens me." Notice the great importance of emphasizes on doing all things through Jesus Christ which strengthens Paul. The source of Paul's strength was Jesus who enabled him to do all things possible and impossible. Jesus is the same source of powerful energy that enables his people to do all things and even achieve the impossible dream such as Barack Obama.

A black minority President in the land of North America inhabited by whites who are the majority race in the country is truly a divine act of God, for the Bible states God establishes kings on the thrones and removes them from office. Barack Obama was selected and chosen by God to lead our country, but before he could become the first black president here on earth God had to establish it first in heaven. He had a divine appointment set up by God.

For God prepared him politically and academically on the backburners of life, so he could walk into his divine destiny just as God prepared King David in the Old Testament for battle against the giant Goliath and to become King over the nation of Israel.

In the New Testament, Jesus taught his disciples one day how to pray by saying "Our Father which are in heaven, Hallowed be thy name. Thy Kingdom come, <u>thy will be done in</u> <u>earth, as it is in heaven</u>". This implies God's will be done in the earth as it is (already done) in heaven.

Not only do I now understand the full meaning of this scripture, but also what Jesus told his disciples when he stated "Whatsoever you loose on earth (when you pray) shall be loosed in heaven." God answered Obama prayer request to be President of the United States on earth as it was established by God in heaven.

In the book of John ch.19 verse 10-11, a Roman governor of the province of Judea, where Jerusalem was located, by the name of Pontius Pilate stated to Jesus "Don't you know that I have the power (or authority) to crucify you and have the power to release you? Notice the quick response of Jesus in the following verse 11, "Thou (you) could have no power (or authority) at all against me, except it were given thee (you) from above."

Pilate thought his claim to power and to have the authority over people was self-doing, but Jesus let him know that the source of his real power and authority came from above. The powers of authorities are given from heaven above such as kings, presidents, and governors according to the book of Romans ch.13 verse 1, for "the powers that be are ordained of God".

All of the three men, I mention earlier President Obama, King David, and the Apostle Paul are just ordinary men doing the impossible by the hand of God. However, Jesus was not an ordinary human being, but the super ordinary Son of God that lived on this earth and fulfilled the will of God as the Son of man.

The Son of man was an extraordinary title that Jesus used to describe himself and label himself as being fully human, so what did President Obama, King David, the Apostle Paul, and Jesus the Christ have in common? All of them have one thing in common and that is their humanity.

They are all human men, and as I stated from the out start of this book the number six in the bible represented the number for man and the serpent, for man and the serpent was created on the sixth day of creation according to the King James Bible of the book of Genesis ch.1 verse 27 and 31.

In the New Testament, there were six water pots of stone that Jesus used to turn natural water into fermented wine at a marriage reception located in the book of John ch.2 verse 6. The six water pots could easily represent man in this first miracle performed by Jesus, for man is just an ordinary vessel filled with regular H2O (water), which represents the human spirit, until divine intervention causes the ordinary water in man's life to turn into a bubbly well of great tasting wine filled with joy.

Now wonder why Jesus stated in John ch.10 verse 10 that "I am come that they (men) might have life and that they (men) might have it more abundantly". The abundant life of Jesus begins with man after his acceptance of the lifestyle of Christ in exchange for his own lifestyle. Most people argued and believed that life began at conception and some people believe life begins at birth. However, I believe life actually starts after the acceptance of eternal salvation by making Jesus as Lord and Savior, and the number eighteen represents the number for life as well as bondage in the Bible.

If a person took the number six that represents man in the Bible and added to it another six, it would equal twelve. The number twelve in the Bible stands for the perfection of government of God's people or the church, for in the Old Testament there were the twelve tribes of Israel and in the New Testament there were the twelve disciples. Add another six to the number twelve, and it would equal the number eighteen which represents the number for bondage, for in the book of Luke ch.13 verse 11, Jesus healed a woman with a spirit of infirmity that had her bent over for 18 years. Also, according to the book of Revelation, 666 is the accumulative number of the mark of the beast and numerical meaning of the anti-Christ or the serpent.

Let's take it one step further and add another six to the number eighteen and it would be equivalent to the number 24. In the book of Revelation ch.4 verse 4, it states that there are 24 seats or thrones surrounding God's throne and 24 elders sitting on them clothed in white raiment wearing on their heads crowns of gold.

The 24 elders show us they symbolize all the past, present, and future saints who are a part of God's wonderful family plus all the redeemed of the Lord that will be worshipping him in heaven together in harmonious unity.

The complete body of Christ gather together in one eternal fellowship is God's ultimate spiritual goal. One goal, one family, one body, one voice, and one sound in heaven will make everything complete with God's eternal master plan. The number for completion in the bible is the number seven or the number of perfection.

In the Old Testament, in the book of Genesis, the book of beginnings, God created the world in six days and rested on the seventh day. God did not rest and relax on the seventh day because he was exhausted and tired from working, but he rested on the seventh day for his work was fully completed and perfect.

In the New Testament, in the book of John ch.17 verse 4, Jesus declared "I have glorified thee (God the Father) on the earth; I have finished (completed) the work which thou (you) gave me to do". Jesus stated he completed the work on earth his Father gave him to do before he went to the cross and die, but on the cross before he finally died he verbally stated it is finished, so the answer to the question can believers complete the work or the will of God in their lifetime before they die is "Yes we Can!"

CHAPTER SEVEN

"What is it or (his will) for Jesus?"

I want to start off chapter seven with the closing of chapter six by clarifying the verbal statement of Jesus on the cross "It is Finished!" Whenever I read this statement in the bible by Jesus, I always wanted to know what "It" was. Most bible readers would interpreted the word "It" by being all of the assigned work God the Father gave Jesus to do on earth, or the ultimate fulfillment of Old Testament prophetic scriptures, but there is also glowing in the dark more illuminate revelation to the word "It" that I want to discuss in this entire chapter.

The word "It" from "It is Finished!" from the book of John ch.19 verse 30 is not only all the work of God the Father had in store for Jesus to accomplished on earth, but the word "It" is the will of God the Father as "the Father's Business", for his only begotten Son to die on the cross. The work and the will of God the Father that Jesus had to complete on earth were two different assignments.

All of the work of God the Father for Jesus to accomplished and perform on earth were all the miracles of healing the sick and the broken hearted, preaching and teaching the gospel to the poor and preaching deliverance to the captives, setting freedom or liberty to them that are bruised, raising the dead, casting out devils, recovering sight to the blind, restoring the lame to walk and causing the mute to talk. So in essence, the work of God the Father occupy the days and the time of Jesus while he lived on the earth,

In Rick Warren's book, "The Purpose Driven Life", he describes the work of Jesus as a balanced life, for he prepared his disciples to live for God's purposes. Rick stated Jesus help his disciples know and love God through worship and taught them to love each other through fellowship and gave them the perfect Word of himself, so they could grow to maturity through discipleship. Also, Jesus showed his disciples how to serve effectively in ministry and sent them out on a mission to inform others. Rick stated that this was the "work" that brought glory to God.

However, the will of God the Father for his son Jesus can be found in the Old Testament book of Isaiah ch.53 verse 10. The King James version reads "Yet it pleased the Lord (God the Father) to bruise him (Jesus the Son). He (God the Father) has put him (Jesus) to grief: when thou (God the Father) shall make his (Son) soul an offering for sin." The following verse number eleven states He (God the Father) shall see of the travail of his (Son) soul, and shall be satisfied: by his (God the Father) knowledge shall my righteous servant justify many; for he (Jesus) shall bear their iniquities." The New International Version by Zondervan gives a clearer understanding by stating "Yet it was the Lord's (God the Father) will to crush him (Jesus) and cause him (the Son) to suffer and the Lord (the Father) makes his (Son's) life a guilt (sin) offering."

God the Father's will for his Son's life on the cross was wrath, punishment, and justice for all because of all the sins humanity committed on this earth. In other words, God the Father's will for Jesus was to suffer and die on the cross, for this is one of the main reasons why Isaiah the prophet is known as the eagle eye, golden tongue prophet who could foresee and foretell the future of Jesus as the Suffering servant. The will and the work of God the Father were both fully completed by Jesus, and I thank and praise the eternal Father for it, because I believe one could not be accomplished without the other.

For example, if Jesus would of completed the will of God the Father only by dying on the cross without doing the work of performing all of the miracles as well as preaching and teaching first then probably a large population of humanity would not have believe or accepted the freedom of his salvation (Read John ch.4 verse 48). Also, vice versa, if Jesus completed all of the work of God the Father only and chose not to do the will of his Father by dying on the cross then humanity would have no redemption.

Both, the will and all the work of God the Father was of great importance and absolutely necessary for Jesus to complete on this earth for the sake of humanity. The heaviest responsibility for a person to carry on his or her shoulders is the weight of sins of the entire world. This responsibility from God the Father was so great that in the book of Luke ch.22 verse 42, Jesus struggled with his own flesh to fulfilled his life's calling in the Garden of Gethsemane by saying "Father, if thou (you) be willing, remove this cup (of suffering and death) from me, nevertheless not my will, but thy (will) be done."

In verse 44 of the same chapter, Jesus is in great agony "and his sweat was as it were great drops of blood falling down to the ground." The heavy burden and pressure of redeeming the entire human race was very costly. It cost Jesus his entire life here on earth.

To many believers, Jesus is known as the Burden bearer or even the Royal cup-bearer (Read the book of Nehemiah), for in past biblical times a cup-bearer's job was to drink and taste the king's wine first before the king would drink it to make sure it was not poisoned by the king's enemies.

The wine taster or cup-bearer was not only a loyal subject, but he also had a dangerous job inside the royal kingdom for sometimes the cup-bearer lived and sometimes the cup-bearer died. Jesus, the Royal cup-bearer asked God the Father (the Royal King) in prayer if he was willing to remove this cup of suffering and death at the cross from him. For all things were and are possible with God the Father, but I noticed the ending of the prayer request by Jesus as he stated not as I will or want for my life, but as thy (you) want.

I believe Jesus was basically saying I know it is my job duty and divine destiny along with purpose to drink from the cup of suffering and death as the royal cup-bearer, but Heavenly Father if you wanted too and are willing to remove this certain particular cup from my possession, please do so. For I know it's full of harmful contents such as poisonous sin, but I fully want to do, as a loyal subject, whatever you decide and whatever is best for me to do for you.

God the Father did not remove this cup from his Son's possession or replaced the cup of suffering and death at the cross with something else. Jesus fully submitted his life to God the Father's will plus accepted the cup of poisonous sins and drunk it completely as his Father wanted for the sake of humanity.

The outcome of the situation for Jesus, the Royal cup-bearer, of course was death, but his death was not in vain, for in his death he justified (declared righteous) many people who believe in him and accepted him as Lord and Savior.

In closing, Jesus completed three major things in his life while he lived on earth. First, he demonstrated as the Son of man, as a physical human being, the expression of God's unconditional love by the perfection of his life through the fulfilment of the law, and second he performed <u>the work</u> of a balanced life with the working of miracles as well as preaching and teaching the Gospel. Third, he completed <u>the will</u> of God the Father with obedience and submission in his life.

As Christian believers, there are three major things in our life that must be completed as well while living on earth and that is being people of love, people of faith, and people of action (good works).

CHAPTER EIGHT

"A Still Small Voice Told Me"

People who have been declared righteous by Christ from their past, present, and future sins are now people of love, faith, and action. For after a person has repented of their sins and accepted by faith the sacrificial life of Jesus on the cross, he or she is forgiven and their sins are not only forgiven but forgotten and erased forever. This person is given a fresh start and a new beginning plus becomes a new creature in Christ; old things are passed away; behold, all things are become new according to Second Corinthians ch.5 verse 17.

God is a God of new beginnings, for in the book of Isaiah ch.43 verse 18-19 declares "Remember you not the former things; neither considers the things of old. Behold, I will do a new thing." The number for new beginnings in the bible is the number eight which is one of my favorite numbers because the number eight is the day I was born on in the six month of June.

Also, the number eight stands for Alpha, for in the book of Revelation the unveiling or disclosure of the secrets of Jesus

Christ, the apostle John reveals in ch.1 verse 8 that God is Alpha (number 8) the beginning and Omega (number 9) the ending.

I will discuss the full meaning of the number nine later in chapter nine. However, I want to maintain focus on the number eight of this chapter "A still small voice told me." One of my favorite stories in the Bible is found in the Old Testament whereas the prophet Elijah was running for his life because he receive a death threat. The king of Israel at this time was Ahab, but his wife, the queen named Jezebel, issued a death warrant to Elijah because he destroyed her 450 false pagan prophets of Baal. After Elijah fled from Queen Jezebel because of her death message, he hid himself inside a cave and dwell in his present sorrows of self-pity.

In 1st Kings Ch. 19 verses 11-12, God commanded Elijah to "Go forth (out of the cave), and stand upon the Mount Horeb (the mountain of God) before the Lord, and behold the Lord passed by and a great and strong wind (maybe a tornado) rent (tore into) the mountains, and broke in pieces the rocks before the Lord; but the Lord was not in the wind: and after the wind an earthquake; but the Lord was not in the earthquake (or in the earthquake of Haiti as some people would presume) and after the earthquake a fire; but the Lord was not in the fire (even though He is a consuming fire): and after the fire a still small voice."

Earth, wind, and fire sounds like the singing group of the 1970's, but God nor his voice were in none of the natural displays or physical disasters. However, a delicate whispering voice is God's voice, and I believe Elijah knew that the sound of gentle whisper was God's voice.

I also believe Elijah realized that God does not reveal himself only in powerful miraculous ways, but he can be revealed and found often gently whispering in the quietness of a humbled human heart.

I remember a person once asked me what did God's voice sounds like. I explained to him one time I heard his voice sound like a multitude of many waters, and many times I hear his voice through the direction of the Holy Spirit, but most of the time I hear his voice echoing softly through his written word (the Bible) reminding me of what he said within my spirit.

This took some time for me as well as a trained ear to hear God's voice, for I learned a secret from Isaiah the prophet found in the book of Isaiah ch.50 verse 4, "God wakened (me) morning by morning, he wakened mine ear to hear as the learned".

First of all, God never sleeps nor slumber according to Psalm 121 verse 4, and if you maintain a constant relationship with him he will sometimes awaken you from your sleep early in the morning to converse with you. There have been plenty of times when God has interrupted my sleeping schedule.

It seems to me that most of the time God wants me at inconvenient times and awkward hours of the night. When times are convenient, and I'm ready to do his will I very seldom hear from him, but when times are inconvenient for me God says lets go its sacrificial time. It's like God is moving me from out of the comfort zone of life. He makes sure I'm uncomfortable with my walk with him, so I don't become stagnant and predictable with my regular routine patterns and sleeping schedules.

One thing I notice from reading the scriptures is God is never at a standstill, for he is seen in his Son's life constantly moving from city to city, performing many miracles, teaching about the kingdom, and working tirelessly in his terrestrial body. God is always on the move plus constantly working, and this is seen in the book of John ch.5 verse 17 of the King James Version where Jesus said "My Father worked hitherto, and I work".

The NIV translation states "My Father never stops working, so why should I?' The work of the Lord is an ongoing process, and believers work not to become saved for that is legalism, but believers work for God by recruiting new comers into his kingdom because they are saved. For the work and the will of God the Father has already been fully completed by Jesus Christ.

I also noticed God interrupted my regular sleeping schedule, so I could become sensitive to his voice and irregular to his ways of doing things. I don't complain about God's interruptions in the middle of the night, for he is teaching me about true ministry and how to reconstruct people lives.

The entire Bible are real divine true stories about God building families and rebuilding people's character as well as their faith. Rebuilding people lives is very hard work plus it is mostly inconvenient at times for ministers, and it requires a great deal of patience. People minds, hearts, and lives are like building small sand castles at a beach. For most of the time right after the sand castles are almost fully completed, a gigantic tidal wave comes in and destroys everything that took time to build.

Many times the tidal waves of life are sent by the enemy, the adversary, the roaring lion known as the devil, for the bible says in the book of Isaiah ch.59 verse 19, "When the enemy shall come in like a flood, the (Holy) Spirit of the Lord shall lift up a standard against him".

Sometimes the tidal waves are a direct result from the storms of life that causes a high tide to enter in and cause water damage to the castle. The outer physical body or the outer shell of people can be similar to small or large sand castles, for some castles are partially damage by the tidal waves while others castles are fully damage.

The beach represents the world from which we live in, and in the book of John ch.16 verse 33, Jesus said "In the world you shall have tribulation but be of good cheer, because I have overcome the world." Rebuilding people lives in this world plus rebuilding large or small sand castles on the beach takes a lot of time and patience, especially after being partially or fully damage by the tidal waves of life.

In the book of Matthew ch.7 verse 24, Jesus said a wise man will build his house upon a rock and not on sand. I have two questions to ask and the first is where does one find a lot of sand at? Of course, the beach! The second question is what is the still small voice of Jesus really saying? He is basically saying do not build your life on the sinking quick sand of this world, but build your life upon the solid rock of him.

The Rock of ages is one of many names that believers call Jesus, but I love to call him the Rock that is filled with milk and honey. It's amazing even now to hear this still small voice whispering in my spiritual ear telling me what to jot down as you read the spiritual information inside this chapter.

In the book of John ch.10 verses 4-5, Jesus said "my sheep follow me, for they know my voice and a stranger will they not follow, but will flee (or run) from him; for they know not the voice of strangers."

The voice of Jesus is speaking a sweet and gentle small whispering sound in my ear saying his sheep or followers recognize his voice mostly through his word which is the Bible, and the voice of strangers (demons) or the voice of the enemy (the devil), which are unfamiliar voices, they (Christians) do not follow or listen to.

Spiritual education and awareness are two essentials keys to believers for helping them to identify voice recognition and discovering the will of God for their lives. Recognizing God's voice from the voice of the enemy can be simple and practical, for God's voice will never tell his followers to say, think, or do something that contradicts his word.

For example, the book of Matthew ch.5 verse 44, Jesus said "Love your enemies," which is God's voice echoing through his word, however; the voice of God would not turn around and say hate your enemies or kill your enemies, for that's not only a contradiction but also a voice of confusion.

According to 1st Corinthians ch.14 verse 33, "God is not the author of confusion, but of peace", so if God is the author of peace, and the author as well as finisher of our faith, according to Hebrews ch.12 verse 2, then the author of confusion is the devil. There are people living in this world that confuse themselves by listening to the voice of the enemy instead of hearing the voice of God through his Word or the voice of the Holy Spirit.

The devil always uses the power of suggestion to say the direct opposite of what God said. God says through King David in the book of Psalm 139 verse 14, "I am fearfully and wonderfully made," and God loves you just the way you are and sent his son Jesus to die for you. The devil your enemy will lie and suggest to you that you are fat and ugly and nobody loves you.

God says in the book of Philippians ch.4 verse 13 "(Yes) you can do all things through Christ which strengthens you, but the enemy says "no you can't!" God says in the book of Proverbs ch.18 verse 21, "Life and death are in the power of the tongue," and words have the power to create plus you can have whatever you say or whatever you say you can have. However, the enemy will say "shut up and be quiet because you are making a fool out of yourself!"

God says in the book of Philippians ch.4 verse 8, "Finally, brethren, whatsoever things are true, whatsoever things are honest, whatsoever things are just, whatsoever things are pure, whatsoever things are lovely, whatsoever things are of good report; if there be any virtue, and if there be any praise, <u>think on these things</u>, but the enemy will suggest think on pornography, the love of money, drugs, sex, and lies.

God says in the book of Hebrews ch.10 verse 35, "Cast not away therefore your confidence which have great recompense of reward", yet the devil not only questions your confidence but strongly suggests throwing it away because it's of little use. However, even Marcus Garvey once stated "If you have no confidence in self, you are twice defeated in the race of life, but with confidence you have won the race even before you have started."

God says in the book of Proverbs ch.23 verse 7, "For as he (a man or woman) thinks in his heart, so is he (or she), and if you think you are somebody like Jesse Jackson use to proclaim "I am somebody!" full of potential and successful then you are, but the enemy lies and states "you are a nobody full of no potential and a complete failure."

God says in the book of John ch.14 verse one, "Let not your heart be troubled: you <u>believe</u> in God, <u>believe also in me</u>" (Jesus), but the enemy says "Don't believe! Especially in Jesus, so I want to close this chapter with a question, and the question is which still small voice are you listening too and obeying?

CHAPTER NINE

§ §

"Not a Fad Five"

The book of Ecclesiastes ch.3 verses 1 & 2 says, "To everything there is a season, and a time to every purpose under the heaven. A time to be born, and a time to die." These verses of scripture let's all of us know that everything in life comes to an end. Every book in the public library that a person reads has a final chapter, and every play as well as every movie shown on Television or in the theaters comes to a final scene. Over a period of time every engine inside a brand new car that is purchase will eventually drive its last mile.

During the four seasons of winter spring, summer, or fall, people lives have unfortunately came to an end. Death is inevitable for people, and it is also consider an enemy of the people, but the Bible says in 1st Corinthians ch.15 verse 26, "the last enemy that shall be destroyed is death". As powerful as death is even death will come to a complete end, and the headlines of every tabloid newspaper worldwide will read "The Death of Death."

I stated it earlier, the number nine in the Bible represents the end or the ending, for God said in the book of Isaiah ch.46 verse

10, he is "declaring the end from the beginning", and a good example of this is seen in the life of Nelson Mandela who was incarcerated in a South Africa prison for 27 years and then was released. The number of years of his entire sentence was 27, but if a person separated the number two from the number seven and then added the numbers together then the number would equal the value of number nine.

Nelson Mandela served 27 years in prison, but his prison sentence finally came to an end which happens to be the same number when added together to the number nine. Some Bible Scholars suggested that Job, from the book of Job, was in his trial and many tribulations for nine months. The number nine is a biblical numerology for visitation or the significant finality as an end to a thing, for right after Mandela's prison sentence came to a complete end, he became a worldwide known celebrity whether or not he wanted to be one.

His life's story reminds me of Joseph in Genesis chapter 41 for right after Joseph was wrongfully accused and released from an Egyptian prison, God exalted him to be the prime minister of Egypt, the second in command to King Pharaoh. God exalted Joseph to a great position of honor, and I believe God exalted Nelson Mandela to a position of great status.

The celebrity status of Nelson Mandela received worldwide attention, for many people looked at him as a worldly celebrity, however I believe the entire world should have considered him as a Christian celebrity.

Saint Augustine once stated "An unjust law is no law at all" and Mandela's faith to endure the 27 years of prison injustice in his country made him a world renowned figure. Not everyone in the body of Christ can be a Christian celebrity if it is such an actually word, for the word itself sounds like an oxymoron.

A Christian friend of mine named Craig Gibson once informed me that a famous televangelist preacher was seen in public and whenever or wherever people noticed him instead of asking him to pray for them, they were asking him for his autograph. There are no big I's and little u's in the body of Christ, for the Apostle Paul teaches from 1st Corinthians ch.12 verse 20 that now "there are many members (and different functions of ministry), but there is only one body."

For example, in the game of basketball in the NBA there are five major starting players in the starting lineup for each team; however, there are also other important minor active role players that come off the bench during the game, but they are all still part of the same team. I believe in the body of Christ the five major players in the starting lineup of building God's kingdom comes from Ephesians ch.4 verse 11 which are apostles, prophets, evangelists, pastors, and teachers.

The apostles are the point guards who spread the gospel or brought us the gospel and pointed us to Jesus. The prophets are the shooting guards who shoot- up and down the sin in our lives as well as the lives of the children of Israel in the Bible. The evangelists are the small forwards who carries and moves the gospel forward from city to city. The teachers are the power forwards who constantly teach us the powerful Word of God every day. The pastors who are the tall centers of attention, for their job is to make sure the devil and his team mates do not score any points over the entire team which is the church.

These apostles, prophets, evangelists, pastors, and teachers are the five starting players of the starting lineup of the gospel team which I usually like to call the fad five or the five-fold ministry.

My question to the reader is what if you are not a fad five or called to be in the starting lineup? What office of ministry should you do? I have wonderful news for you as an important active church minor role player. I spoke about NBA role players coming off the bench to play inside a basketball game.

In the NBA, there is an award called the sixth man award given to one of the best players coming off the bench who provides consistent high energy and a spark to help their team win. This award is for bench role players only and it is not available for members of the starting lineup.

Once an off the bench minor role player has achieve this award in the NBA, it is consider a great accomplishment and achievement for that player. For if an injury occurs to one of the fad five starting members of the team then the head coach usually substitute the injured player, for the player that received the sixth man player award.

Most of the head coaches in the NBA implement the sixth man into the starting rotation until the starting player returns from his injury, but sometimes the position can be permanent if the injury is career threatening, or if the starting player returns from his injury and becomes less productive to help his team win due to his injury.

I stated all of this to say that in the one body of Christ, Almighty God is the head coach in the game of life and most of the fad five operated from the five-fold ministry. If God as the head coach takes a time out and calls one of the fad five out of the game to get some rest by sitting him or her on the bench in heaven, the sixth man will be the one to fill in and help God's team or kingdom from losing lost souls in the battle of life.

An example of this is when God called the general of the gospel G.E. Patterson home to be with him in heaven. I remember thinking to myself who can possibly mirror him as an individual preacher and run his church as well as fulfill his shoes. I then thought to myself, whoever it is has some pretty big shoes to fill, for the Bible states in Romans ch.10 verse 15, "how beautiful are the feet of them that preach the gospel of peace and bring glad tidings of good things."

Even though G.E. Patterson's feet were gorgeously beautiful, whoever took over his church assignment as pastor still had some pretty big shoes to fill, however God was not looking for a person to wear a bigger size to replace him, but for someone to come off the bench and wear the same size in his shoes of faith.

Jesus said in the book of John ch.12 verse 31, "Now shall the prince of this world (the devil) be cast out and I, if I (Jesus) be lifted up from the earth (by the cross), (I) will draw all men unto me" (to be saved from their sins and have eternal life). From this scripture alone, Jesus declared he already won the war between him and the devil at the cross and we have the victory, for Satan the devil is a defeated foe and his destiny is the lake of fire and brimstone, according to the book of Revelations ch.20 verse 10.

The devil, beast, and false prophet will be tormented in the lake of fire forever and ever, however until this time comes into fulfillment, the war is over. For Jesus won it at the cross of cavalry, but the battle for human souls is still at large. The battle between good and evil still exist in life here on earth and many lieutenants, generals, sergeants, plus soldiers die on the battle field of life and that's why God still has recruiters recruiting for his army.

What does NCAA college football and basketball and the NFL as well as the NBA have in common? They all have recruiters recruiting new members for their schools or teams. This is mainly my job duty or responsibility somewhat similar to the sixth man role of the NBA, recruiting, drafting, and training new members to come join in God's army and fight the enemies of darkness through the Word of God, prayer, praise, and worship. When my life comes to a complete end, I hoped to achieve the sixth man award received from God.

In closing of this chapter, the Bible states that "Many are called, but Few are chosen" and even if you have not been chosen or selected to be one of the fad five or operated in the five-fold ministry. However, you and I are both called to the office of ministry of helps and reconciliation helping to advance God's glorious kingdom throughout the earth as a faithful steward of Jesus Christ.

CHAPTER TEN

§ §

"What is God's will for us?"

In the book of John ch.14 verses 1 and 2 it states, "Let not your heart be troubled, you believe in God, believe also in me. "In my Father's **house** are **many mansions** (or many rooms the size of mansions, but only one house), if it were not so, I would have told you, I go to prepare a place for you". **Jesus is the master builder** of this heavenly city and **heaven** is **a prepared place** for **a prepared people** just as **hell** is **a prepare place** of everlasting fire for **unprepared** lost unbelieving people (see Matt. ch.25 verse 41). If a person chooses to go to heaven, he or she must prepare during this lifetime, but if a person chooses to go to hell it's because he or she lacked preparation.

Earth is the place making ready the wise people in preparation to meet the Lord in heaven. This place is a better perfect place that Jesus refers to. Heaven is a better place than earth like love is better than hatred, good is better than evil, light is better than darkness when it comes to seeing, the Holy Spirit is better than the human spirit, God is better than Satan, and better is better than being bitter. God created earth as a wonderful place for humans to live, and his invisible glory is physically seen throughout creation, for creation itself reveals our Creator's glory, but as earth is a beautiful site of his glorious creation, heaven will be much greater.

According to the book of Revelation ch.21 verses 16-21, the city of Heaven is shaped like a rubric's cube and this means that it is either a cube or a pyramid.

I believe it is a perfect cube or at least has the base of a perfect cube, and it is the same shape as the Most Holy Place in Solomon's Temple of the Old Testament (1 Kings ch.6 verse 20). God made and formed earth in the shape of a circle, but heaven lies four-squared and prepared like a clear golden square of six equal sides. This heavenly celestial city is made of pure clear gold and the streets are paved with clear gold and some books with the printing inside and outside are covered in gold.

Each of the twelve magnificent gates of heaven is made of a single solid pearl and at the gates twelve angels. The building of the city wall is made of jasper, but its constructional foundations are garnished and inlaid with twelve different kinds of precious gemstones. There is a splendorous house where the rooms inside the house are the size of mansions unnumbered, plus white horses as well as white glistening robes wore by angels and by the citizens of heaven.

In the book of Isaiah ch.55 verses 9-10, God said "my thoughts are not your thoughts, neither are your ways my ways, says the Lord. "For as the heavens are higher than the earth, so are my ways higher than your ways, and my thoughts than your thoughts." God's thoughts and ways are higher than our thoughts and ways here on earth, and he said the heavens are higher than the earth.

Since heaven is a lot higher than earth, it has a better, perfect higher quality, and quantity of scenery than earth. Think about earth's beautiful scenery, the green grass of all the fields, the red, white, yellow, violet flowers that grow in the fields, the different shapes, colors and sizes of fruits, vegetables, and animals that lived on the fields. Earth has amazing blue skies and large deep oceans with white puffy clouds and white sand beaches.

Also, there are the glorious lights shining from the brightness of sun by day and the moon as well as the stars glowing by night. Earth is a painted picture canvas by God, but heaven will be a better fully perfect completed place.

The number for full and total completion in the Bible is the number ten, or the perfection of divine order.

Jesus said in his Father's house which is in heaven has many rooms, but in order to receive full access inside the rooms, the size of mansions in heaven, Christians must first <u>learn</u> and <u>do</u> the will of God the Father on earth. He also declare in Matthew ch.7 verse 21, "Not everyone that says unto me, Lord, Lord, shall enter into the kingdom of heaven, but he that <u>doeth the will of my Father</u> which is in heaven".

What is the will of God the Father for us? I believe his will for the many spiritual infants and adults that are called can be found in the book of St. John ch.6 verse 40 and also located from the infant Thessalonian church in 1st Thessalonians ch.4 verse 3 and ch.5 verses 16-18.

The King James Version of John ch.6 verse 40 declares, "This is the will of him (the Father) that sent me that everyone which see the Son (Jesus), and believe on him, may have everlasting life, and I will raise him up at the last day."

The Bible commentary of Matthew Henry states the Father's will for us is to believe on Jesus, repent of our sins, live a holy life, love one another, and sanctification. Physical bodily sanctification is very important to God, for according to 1st Thessalonians 4:3, it specifically states "For this is the will of God, even your sanctification, that ye (you) should abstain from fornication" which is pre-marital sex.

However, in order to abstain from pre-marital sex, high concentration levels of one's full attention or mental effort should focus on the activity response of these next three important steps then one would actually find himself or herself doing or fulfilling the will of God for their lives as babes in Christ. "For out of the mouth of babes, God has ordained perfect praise" (Matt.21:16).

According to 1st Thessalonians 5:16-18, the three important steps are "Rejoice evermore, pray without ceasing, and in everything give thanks, for (or because) this is the will of God in Christ Jesus concerning you".

God's will for us is to love one another, abstain from fornication (pre-marital sex), rejoice evermore, (not that the spirits are subject unto you through his name, but rejoice because your names are written in heaven- Luke10:20) pray and give thanks always. Doing God's will is just putting these simple three steps into practice on a daily basis, and it can be done as easy as it sounds if one lives a discipline lifestyle like this every day.

By performing these three steps daily many Christians will enter into the kingdom of heaven and stand in the presence of an Almighty God forever as the many that are called. Remember the few that are chosen is consider the fad five, but the many that are called are called to do the will of the Father.

A good example of this can be found in the book of Numbers ch.17 verses 1-10. In this chapter, God told Moses to take twelve rods, according to the twelve tribes of Israel, and write on each rod every man's name representing their father's tribe and place the twelve rods inside the Tabernacle of the most Holy of Holies in front of the Ark of the Covenant.

God said to Moses, buds will sprout on the rod belonging to the man that he chooses to minister before him and his people. After all the twelve rods, representing the twelve tribes of Israel, were placed in the presence of God, the very next day Moses found that Aaron's rod representing the tribe of Levi had sprouted, blossomed, and produced almonds.

When Moses brought all the rods out from the Lord's presence, he showed them to the people of Israel and each man claimed his own rod. God then told Moses to place Aaron's rod permanently inside the Ark of the Covenant to be kept as a token against the rebels of Israel. This story represents the many twelve tribes that were all called, but only one tribe was chosen to minister before the Lord's presence as well as the people presence (public ministry –the Fad Five).

Aaron was a descendent of the tribe of Levi who were the Levitical priesthood of Israel that was chosen to be God's ministers. Aaron's rod plus the eleven other rods were ordinary wooden staffs which were made from dead tree branches. The wood itself of the twelve wooden staff's, and the wood of the Ark of the Covenant represented humanity. The overlaying of gold on the inside and outside of the Ark of the Covenant represented divinity plus the Ark itself represented Jesus, the Son of God. The contents inside the Ark of the Covenant were Aaron's rod, a jar of manna, and the Ten Commandments.

The dead wooden tree branch of Aaron's rod that budded represents the resurrection. The manna (or bread) inside the jar represented God's provision for his people and the Ten Commandments represented the law of God. Jesus said he is the resurrection and life as the true bread which came down from heaven as well as Jehovah Jireh our great provider. He also stated in the book of Matthew ch.5 verse 17, he did not come to destroy the law, but to fulfill the law. The Old Testament writings and sayings of the OT prophets and every law of the Ten Commandments were fulfilled by Jesus, so as his eternal reward for fulfilling the law on earth, he is now reunited in heavenly glory with God the Father.

Jesus now sits on the right hand throne of God, for Psalm 15 verse 11 states that in God's presence is the fullness of joy, so I believe not only is the fullness of joy in God's presence, but the fullness of peace, love, and everlasting life.

All of the twelve wooden staff's that represented the many tribes of Israel were placed in God's presence overnight, but only one Levi tribe or the fad five as one team was selected to minister and lead while the rest of the many eleven were called to listen and to follow.

In closing, to the many lost children of unbelievers, spiritual infants and adults in Christ that are not called as one of the fad five, but are called as many to follow the example of Jesus by loving one another, abstaining from pre-marital sex, rejoicing evermore, praying without ceasing (stopping), and in everything give thanks to God, "for this is the will of God in Christ Jesus concerning you."

The most important lesson one can take and learn from the twelve wooden staff's that represented humanity is to abide or remain and live in God's presence not only overnight, but every day and every night, then the dying wooden staff of all our human bodies will also experience the budding, sprouting, resurrecting almond power of Jesus Christ, "for in him we live, and move, and have our (essence of) being" (Acts ch.17:28).

CHAPTER ELEVEN

"Every Knee will Bow and many will Say"

Some people believe Heaven is eleven, but the number eleven does not stand for Heaven in the Bible because the number eleven stands for confusion. As stated in the last chapter, the number ten is the number for the full divine order of God, but the number eleven means disorder or confusion.

Also, the number forty is the number that represents generations and in this godless generation or dispensation of government generations, whereas the author and finisher of fear and confusion is the devil. He can be seen operating behind the scenes as the unseen foreman in charge of the construction projects of building a great city which is the tower of Babel located in Genesis ch.11 verse 4.

"For they (the children of men) said, Go to, let us build us a city and a tower, whose top may reach unto heaven; and let us make us a name, lest we be scattered abroad upon the face of the whole earth." This construction project by the children of men was not necessary a bad idea, in fact it was a good idea, for the exception of one major thing it was not a God idea.

It was satan's idea, for the children of men to build this tower as a monument to their own greatness to call attention to their own great human achievement. It was also the devil's idea to establish and gather together ungodly men in unity to bring about an international order. God commended the people for their achievement of unity, but their hidden agenda was very selfish and self-serving, because it was a monument built by and for the people themselves rather than to God.

Over the years, I have built some high towers and monuments in my own personal life such as high paying jobs, expensive cars, and fancy clothes, but I thank God for divine intervention and personally, spiritually interfering in my business to tear them down. The tower of Babel was not only a miraculous structure, but a common structure in ancient times in Babylon (Iraq), and it was most likely a ziggurat.

According to the New Living Translation Life Application Study Bible, Ziggurats were mostly built as temples and looked like pyramids with steps or ramps leading up the sides. They were the focal point of the city because they stood as high as 300 feet and they were often 300 feet wide. By building this tower, the children of men hoped to create an identity name and self-worth that would take God's place in their lives.

Of course, God in his infinite wisdom knew the children of men try to replace him in their lives by attempting to build this monumental tower to the heavens, so he came down from heaven to stop the building of this earthly project.

God was compelled to change their one language into many different languages, so it would destroy their powerful unity. Remember, the number one in the Bible stands for divine unity, but the number eleven stands for confusion as well as a satanic unity.

For example, I hate to bring up the past of painful memories, but I remember when the two twin towers in New York City felled like it was yesterday. The 11th day of the ninth month of September in 2001 was the day satanic terrorist attackers gather themselves together in unity and attacked America's homeland.

The airplane attacks on America soil left all Americans of the United States in a state of confusion. After this major disaster occurred, many Americans including myself were wondering why we were under attack. Many Americans did not know why we were attacked nor had a logical reasonable explanation until President Bush address the matter later on T.V.

However, the attacks on 911 not only cause a state of confusion and disorder for many Americans, but it causes a worldwide panic of fear and anger. Maybe, it was my imagination, but I remember looking at the Twin Towers on T.V. One tower standing beside another tower and to me they looked very similar to the number 11.

The terrorist attackers were like the children of men in Genesis with their hidden agenda to make a great name for themselves in the earth and to call attention to their own personal human achievement. But, they forgot one important detail of the story of the Tower of Babel in God's word which is God destroyed the satanic unity of the children of men by confounding their language and scattering them abroad. Therefore, God will also do away with the satanic unity of terrorist cell groups scatter abroad, for God is a God of love, and not the god of hate.

The god of hate is the devil, for Jesus said in the book of John ch.10 verse 10, the thief (or the chief thief known as the devil) comes to steal, kill, and destroy.

The devil was the unseen foreman of evil operating behind the scenes in charge of the whole construction site project and unity of the terrorist hijackers of 911.

The children of men in Genesis attempted and failed to replace God in their lives with the construction of the Tower of Babel; whereas, the terrorist attackers by committing 911 succeeded and replaced God in their personal lives by the destruction of the Twin Towers.

For this very reason alone, God will hold each person involve in 911 personally accountable and responsible for the death of many innocent people. Terrorist attackers of 911 believed with all their heart that they were doing the will of their god, but my God of the bible states in the book of Matthew ch.7 verses 21-23, "Not everyone that says unto me, Lord, Lord, shall enter into the Kingdom of heaven, but he that doeth the will of my Father which is in heaven. Many will say to me in that (last) day, Lord, Lord, have we not prophesied in thy name? And in thy name have cast out devils? And in thy name done many wonderful works? "And then will I (Jesus) profess unto them (911 attackers, false prophets, false leaders and teachers), I never knew you: depart (to outer darkness) from me, you that work iniquity."

On the last Day of Judgment called the Great White Throne Judgment Day everyone's knee will bow before Jesus, but not everyone that says Lord Jesus will enter into the Kingdom of heaven, for many will question why not. Terrorist attackers will say Lord didn't we cast out white devils in North America by destroying the Twin Towers in New York, and in our eyes do a wonderful work in the name of Allah (God)?

Fake leaders, phony Christian believers, false preachers and teachers of the gospel that prophesied (or preach) in the name of Jesus for money or ill got gain will say Lord, have we not preach in your name and perform the will of God in our lives? Then will Jesus say unto all of them depart from me because I never knew you or I never talk to you, and I never had a one on one personal relationship with you every day through prayer.

Spiritual and physical relationships take a lot of investment of time, for the word knew that Jesus refers to here is to know someone through and over an extensive period of time as one does on an intimate level such as marriage partners, but the word depart means to go away from.

So, Jesus is really saying to them go away from me into a place of outer darkness, for you were workers of iniquity (evil workers of darkness) on earth. God is justified in doing this, for in the book of Genesis, he separated light from darkness, and the workers of darkness should be united with darkness as well as the evil forces of wickedness plus the devil, so they all can be in a satanic unity as one whole evil family of darkness.

Although, satanic unity is seen developing and existing on earth, there is also a divine unity that exists in God's kingdom plus an eleven commandment that Jesus gave to his disciples in the book of John ch.13 verse 34-35. "A new commandment I give unto you, that you love one another; as I have loved you, that you also love one another. By this shall all men know that you are my disciples, if you have love for one another?"

There are Ten Commandments listed in the Old Testament book of Exodus ch.20 starting at verse three, but in the New Testament Jesus adds a new commandment to his disciples to follow also. This is the eleven commandment that Jesus wants all of us to follow which is to love each other.

For love is the glue that keeps divine unity together forever among the brethren. Love keeps brothers sticking together and not fighting or killing each other like Cain and Abel. Cain did not love Abel, but he hated him, for he was jealous of him because God accepted his offering and rejected his. If Cain would of chose love instead of hate, he would not had killed his brother Abel in the field of life.

In the book of Luke ch.15 verse 28, there is another story about a Prodigal son and his older brother who was angry and jealous because of what their Father did for the younger son. Divine unity among the brothers and sisters in Christ is God's one true universal love language that can never be separated by hate or by the confusion of speaking many different languages like at the Tower of Babel.

The Tower of Babel for Christians is heaven where divine unity will be established forever. For "Behold, how good and how pleasant it is for brethren to dwell together in unity! "It is like the precious ointment upon the head that ran down upon the beard even Aaron's beard: that went down to the skirts of his garments (Psalm 133 verses 1 & 2).

The spiritual head of the church is Jesus Christ, but the actual physical body of Christ is the church here on earth made up of many different colorful members in his one body. God is love and his anointing of love travels down from the head of Christ, and the beard of Christ to the (churches) body of Christ bleeding through their fleshy garments like a pleasant aroma of cologne or perfume.

God's fragrance of love, and the eleven commandment is actually the second greatest commandment found in the book of Matthew ch.22 verse 39, which is to "Love your neighbor as you love yourself."

CHAPTER TWELVE

"The God of Impossibilities"

T he most- wisest king that ever lived and ruled on earth in the Old Testament was King Solomon. Jesus was the wisest person that lived in the New Testament for he was the Son of God. According to the book of 1st Kings Ch.4 verse 32, King Solomon composed 3,000 proverbs and wrote 1,005 songs, and he was considered an animal naturalist and plant biologist.

Solomon wisdom was known throughout the ancient world and in all his superior wisdom he wrote in the book of Ecclesiastes ch.11 verse 5, "As thou knows not what is the way of the spirit (the wind) or how the bones do grow in the womb of her that is with child; even so thou knows not the works (or ways) of God who makes all."

King Solomon is basically saying as one does not know the pathway of the wind as far as its directional pattern or whereabouts of its coming and going from its windy storehouse, and the mystery of how the bones of a child grows in its mother's womb. One also does not know the mysterious ways of the Lord or how the Lord works in mysterious ways.

I personally believe that one of the main reasons why God works in strange mysterious ways is to show himself strong by performing miracles as the Invisible Impossible God. For he can do the impossible by making them all possible realities. The greatest showman in heaven and on earth is God. Michael Jordan, Michael Jackson, Mike Tyson, and Muhammad Ali were not the greatest showmen on earth compared to God Almighty, even though they were all great in the field of sports and entertainment.

All throughout the Bible, God did the impossible, so the major theme of this final chapter is God is the God of Impossibilities. Not only is God a miracle worker for impossible missions and conditions, but he is also the God of impossible situations and major circumstances. Throughout the entire Bible, God is basically doing not only the impossible mostly through his son Jesus, and the Apostles in the New Testament, but also through the major prophets of the Old Testament.

In the Bible, God used Moses and Aaron as earthly messengers plus a wooden staff to bring about a display of his great power to Pharaoh of Egypt with ten plagues. To deliver the Israelites out of the hands of the Egyptians when Egypt was considered the first dominant superpower of the ancient world in history was a mission impossible. He did the impossible and showed himself to be very strong plus demonstrated his awesome strength as a great deliverer of slavery to the Israelites, and the Egyptians as well as to the entire world.

God is still a great Deliverer today, for he not only can deliver people from the oppression of slavery for 400 years, but he can deliver the alcoholic from alcoholism of 20 years, the crack addict from the toxic poison of using crack of 10 years, and the prostitutes and drug dealers of soliciting their precious bodies and selling drugs on the street corners for 5 years.

He can deliver the worst sinner from sin and make him or her into the finest saint or missionary for his glory. A wonderful example of this is the Apostle Paul formerly known as Saul of Tarsus. God can also deliver the common white and blue collar thieves from stealing, the constant liars from lying, and the national and internationally known most wanted killers from killing. God can deliver physically, mentally, emotionally, financially, and spiritually.

According to the book of Luke ch.1 verse 37, God can do the impossible, for with God nothing shall (or ever will) be impossible. The Old Testament scriptures in the book of Exodus shows and proves to us today that God can deliver human beings from physical slavery like in the case of the Israelites. The Jewish people led by Moses were not the only race of people deliver from oppression and physical enslavement in foreign territory.

For God also used a black Gentile Moses in the form of Dr. Martin Luther King Jr. as a messenger or spokesman for African Americans to be liberated from physical white supremacy in North America. God not only delivers physically from the bondage of slavery, but he is a great Deliverer, for all those that are tormented mentally from the guilt of their past and demonically tormented with thoughts of suicide.

All of those that are torn emotionally into pieces in their heart as well as suffering from a major financial debt crisis in their lives, God can deliver. The person that needs spiritual deliverance from fictional leaders, false religions, artificial traditions, and fake doctrines of men, once again God is the ultimate Deliverer.

From a Biblical standpoint there is another form of slavery besides physical enslavement and that is spiritual slavery. God used Moses to inform King Pharaoh of Egypt to let his people the Israelites go, so they could come and worship him in the wilderness. God also used Jesus to die on the cross plus serve notice to Satan (the prince and pharaoh of this world), and the spiritual slave master of God's created people to let them go.

So, they could come and worship him for their deliverance from spiritual slavery and sin in the local wilderness which is symbolic to the Church sanctuary.

The book of Colossians ch.1 verse 13 states, "God the Father have delivered us from the power of darkness." A great spokesman by the name of El-Hajj Malik El-Shabazz or better known as Malcolm X once stated with the words of his intelligent black voice "By any means necessary," and the cross that Jesus die on is the only way and means necessary that God the Father intended for spiritual freedom and deliverance of one's own soul.

For Jesus stated in the book of John ch.14 verse 6, "I am the way (and not a way), the truth (and not a lie), and the (eternal) life, no man comes unto (God) the Father, but by me." The only way to escape from Satan and sin (the dark demonic powers that be) is through faith in the death of God's son Jesus, and the shedding of his blood on an old rugged cross.

The key to experience this total fullness of spiritual freedom is faith alone, for according to Hebrews ch.11 verse 6 states "without faith it is impossible to please God". The life of Moses pleased God because he put his faith into action.

After Moses and the Israelites left Pharaoh and the Egyptians in Egypt,

God judged and destroyed King Pharaoh plus his army of foot soldiers in the Red Sea. I often wonder if the blood of the many

Egyptian bodies that drowned in the Red Sea made the sea redder and therefore it was surname the Red Sea.

Before God deliver the Israelites from Egypt, he told Moses in the book of Exodus ch.3 verse 7 that he heard the cry (or prayer) of his people by reason of their taskmasters and then declared to Moses that he knew their sorrows. This moved God with righteous indignation, wrath, vengeance, and judgment upon Egypt.

I want to emphasize a special point in God's divine master plan and purpose after Moses and the Israelites left Egypt after 400 years of physical slavery. If God judged the ancient world of Egypt after Moses and the Israelites left, why should he not judged this modern day world after Jesus returns in the rapture and leaves with his people after being deliver from 2000 years of spiritual slavery?

God visibly showed us through the ten plagues against Egypt in the book of Exodus that he is not just a God over the human race, but he is also the God over nature, and the forces of nature along with controlling the behavior of any insects or animals.

In the Old Testament, the first plague that God performed in Egypt over nature was to turn natural H2O water in the river into blood. In the New Testament, the first miracle God's son Jesus performed in the book of John chapter two was to turn natural pure water into fermented drinking wine at a wedding reception in Cana of Galilee.

In the Old Testament, the seventh plague against Egypt was a major hailstorm, and the hail was mingled with fire from heaven. In the days of Elijah, God did not allow it to rain for three and a half years. In the book of Joshua ch.10 verse 13, God made the sun and the moon stand still for Joshua in the sight of Israel. In the New Testament, in the book of Matthew ch.8 verse 26, Jesus commands the winds and the sea to obey him.

Not only is Jesus the God over nature and controls all of nature forces, but he is the Lord over the laws that govern the Universe such as: the laws of space and time, the laws of gravity, and the laws of medicine and science. In the book of John ch.6 verse 19, the disciples see Jesus walking on water which defies the laws of gravity.

Also, God is a God that can control any insects plus all the animals and their behavior. For in the Old Testament, in the book of Exodus, God spoke to the frogs, the lice, the flies, and the locust to attack Egypt. A Greek scholar by the name of Socrates once stated if an elephant was down that even a small ant would walk over to the elephant and kick it.

Although, I am not declaring that God controlled this ant's behavioral action to attack and kick the elephant, however; I am acknowledging the true and powerful fact that God is able to do it.

In the book of Genesis, God commanded and controlled all the animals including the ants and the elephants to enter Noah's ark before the flood came and to exit the ark after the flood receded. In the book of Daniel ch.6 verse 22, God saved Daniel from the lion's den by shutting the mouths of the lions, so they would not eat or harm Daniel. In the book of Numbers ch.22 verse 28, God spoke to the prophet Balaam through the mouth of a donkey.

In the book of 1st Kings Ch.17 verse 4, God commanded the ravens (birds) to feed his prophet Elijah by the brook before the Jordan River. God is Almighty and the Supreme Being of supernatural unlimited power. He possesses powers beyond measure that the natural human mind cannot even fully embrace to understand or comprehend.

Jesus stated in the book of Mark ch.12 verse 24 to the Sadducees (the religious sect), "You know not the scriptures, neither the power of (Almighty) God." Listen carefully to the voice of Jesus when he said to the Sadducees "You do not know scriptures (God's word) or the power of God" (the Father).

First of all, God's words are powerful, for they are spirit and alive meaning it generates or gives life, so therefore God's power is from his word the Bible.

Second, the book of John ch.1 verse 14 states, "the Word was made flesh (in the form of Jesus Christ) and dwelt among us." The Word was God's son known as Jesus the Christ like John declared in ch.1 verse 1, so Jesus was informing the Sadducees that they don't know the power of God, but he knows it to be basically a never ending creative life force and source of supplies of miracles and wonders mysterious performed by the activation of our faith in him, if we only believe.

Third, God's power is supernatural and not only does he has the power to be the God over nature, nature forces, and the laws of the Universe as well as controlling the behavior of the insects and animals, but he is also the Maker of all metals such as gold, silver, diamonds, gemstones, copper, and all of the wooden objects on earth.

In the book of Haggai ch.2 verse 8, "The silver and gold is mine says the Lord of hosts," and God has the power to multiply these resources and give them to his children, for the book of Hosea ch.2 verse 8 states so.

"For she did not know that I (God) gave her corn, wine, and oil plus multiplied her silver and gold which they prepared for

Baal." The silver and gold that God multiply and gave to Gomer the wife of Hosea is seen here as a shadow type for God's people Israel who prostituted themselves by using the gold and silver to worship a Canaanite pagan god named Baal. God is the giver of all spiritual and natural resources.

There is an accidental story found in 2 Kings Ch.6 verse 6 whereas God made an iron ax head float on top of water. Most of all small heavy pieces of metal objects in water normally sink to the bottom and not swim to the top. Also, in the book of Exodus ch.15 verse 25, God had Moses take a wooden tree branch and throw it into the water of Marah, for the water would not taste bitter but sweet, so the people of Israel could drink from it. Only God can perform these kinds of miracles with ease, for it is a light thing with him.

Look what John the Baptist said in the book of Matthew ch.3 verse 9 when he stated that "God is able (or has the power) of these stones to raise up children unto Abraham." This was a wonderful proclamation of faith announced by John. Ultimately, God can do anything above and beyond what we can ask or think to imagine with our finite human minds.

If I was Jesus's defense attorney before he was convicted to die on the cross in Roman times, I would of cross examined him as a prosecuting witness before the Roman jury and Pilate himself by presenting evidence and the facts of the case that he was completely innocence of all charges, and that he was the Son of God. The evidence was and still is conclusive that Jesus was the Son of God.

Let's look carefully at the evidence and miracles of Jesus before he was crucify. He was seen walking on natural water plus he cleansed a leper from leprosy. He turned water into wine also he calmed the raging wind and sea. He healed a woman with an issue of blood for 12 years, and raised Jairus's 12 year old daughter from the dead.

He restored sight to the blind plus cast out devils into a herd of 2000 pigs. He transfigured himself in front of Peter, James, and John on a high mountain. He curses a fig tree plus feed a multitude of 5000, and 4000 people on two different occasions with a few loaves of bread and fish.

He taught in the synagogues of the Jews with great authority and taught about the kingdom of God and heaven in many parables. He was denied swearing by Peter, betrayed by a kiss with Judas, and after his resurrection doubted by his disciple doubting Thomas.

Jesus rose from the dead three days after he was crucified on the Roman cross, so this was the last and final miracle that he would perform on the earth to prove once and for all that he was and still is alive as the Son of God.

For as the prophet Jonah was in the belly of the great whale for three days and was release unto dry land to preach repentance to the city of Nineveh, so will Jesus stay in the heart of the earth and be release after three days, and then have his twelve disciples preach the gospel of repentance and salvation to the whole world.

No other religions such as: Muslims, Hinduism, Buddhism, and Judaism can claim a person from their religion has fully returned from the dead except Jesus the Christ, the only begotten Son of God, and the Lord of Christianity.

In closing, I want to share one final statement that is mind blowing to me which is in the book of John ch.16 verse 28, the NIV Translations states Jesus said it this way "I came from the

Father, and entered the world; now I am leaving the world and going back to the Father."

I believe like Jesus was with God the Father first, before he was sent from heaven to earth, and from earth to the cross from the cross to the grave, and from the graveyard back to heaven with God his Father. All of us follow this same exact pattern in life as well, as Proverbs 8:27 & 30 says, "I was there when God prepared the heavens and set a circle upon the face of the deep," for "then I was by him, as one brought up with him: and I was daily his delight, rejoicing always before him." Most theologians reference this scripture to Jesus alone, yet I believe we were with God the Father first before we were born and sent from heaven to earth in our natural fleshly bodies, but instead of going to the cross to die for humanity sins like Jesus did, we first deny ourselves and take up the cross of Jesus daily.

For all of us are at the crossroads of life to make a wise choice to follow Jesus or an unwise decision to follow Satan (the god in charge of the temptations of this world), and to be tested and tried by God according to our faith to totally surrender to God's perfect will instead of our own will like Jesus did.

The Bible states in First Peter ch.2 verse 21, Jesus left all of us an earthly example that we should follow his steps in life. The eternal choice is yours for the making to leave the graveyard and return back to God the Father in glory and honor, plus also receive your reward for overcoming the world.

A matter of spiritual fact according to First John ch.5 verse 5, "he that overcomes the world is he that believes that Jesus is the Son of God."

Also, Jesus stated in John ch.16 verse 33, "In the world you shall have tribulation, but be of good cheer, (for) I have overcome the world." Jesus overcame the world through his death, burial, as well as his resurrection, and you can too if you follow him with a pure heart of faith to the end, for the end result will be your eternal reward awaits you in heaven for overcoming the world, and its many challenges plus temptations.

However, the eternal choice is yours, because you have a free will to choose God's will or your own will, and I pray that you choose wisely and select God's perfect will for your life, yet as for me and my household, we shall serve and do the work or will of God the Father through the Lord Jesus forever, for he that do the will of God abide forever (1st John ch.2 verse 17).

SPECIAL ACKNOWLEDGEMENTS

§ &

I would like to give special acknowledgements to my wonderful decease mother Barbara Lopes who raise me with unconditional love and to my sibling brother as well as brother in the gospel Troy Lopes, and to his wife Tonya and their wonderful children.

I give kudos to Troy Jr. and my favorite Aunt Ree and Uncle Harold and to my cousins Rodney, Danny, Kelly, and Dana, Ashely and Kyle, Lisa, Terri, and Sarah. I also give credit to my Uncle John, Paul, David, Joey, Rickey,

Aunt Donna, and Aunt Mary / my mom's best friend.

A special acknowledgement to the trailblazers of the Walton family my grandparents: <u>William Walton</u> and <u>Margaret Walton</u> who both went home to be with the Lord Jesus and whom I will always dearly love and miss as well as my Uncle Billy. To my ex-wife Malinda Smith I thank you for my son D.J. and to his deceased brother Michael Dawson who will never be forgotten as well as my stepdad Matthew Lopes and my biological father Lee Wayne Mann. Also Liz's husband Beans, Newt, Madea, and Grandpa Reese.

To my childhood friends as well as current friends: Lee Blakey, Will Robinson, Kevin & Shervina Burrows, Duane Paige, Lin Alston & Alicia, Spider, Monique, Mike Littleton, Shane & Michael Bell, Meechie and Avery Ervin, Ladonna Miller, Lamar Scales, Tony Bozeman, Tony Trout, Twonne & Sean Hunter and their sister and mother Cookie, Dexter Blunt, Cynthia Preston, Vanessa Poindexter, Brian and Jeff Palmer, Rufus & Donald Morgan, Keith and Luke, Jada McDaniel, Troy Johnson, Jennifer Nelson, Mark Roquemore, Pat Kellum, Josiah Amos and Patricia Amos and the entire Ross family: Neeka, Debbie, Heidi, Corey, Mark, Sable, Adrian, Jimmy Lunsford, Edward, Akili Hutchinson, Floyd Reed, Victor White, Lynn & Ronnie Fryar, Tiffany & Robert Littlejohn, Gerald Montgomery, Rob Meyers, Ronald & Calvin Freeman, Cindy(Boo) Smith and her sister, Cora Strickland, Chaka & Bobbette Chandler, Denise Anthony, Newton Burris, Sean, Norman and Sally Watkins, Marcus & Paula Hall, Lisa, Connie, & Larry Smith.

To my spiritual brothers of the gospel that help me spread the good news on Television: Elder Craig Gibson, Andrew Bryant, Johnny Amos, Marion Kelsor, Tony Towns, Lewis Breaston, Sean Scott, Greg Joiner, Curtis Turner, Orlando Anthony, Mark Matthews. To the supportive wife's of these great ministers Chermelle Gibson, Susan Matthews, Brenda Breaston, Lashaun Amos, Renee Anthony.

To the Godparents of my daughter Diana: Barb and Russ and to my mother in law Carol Shaw-Dabo, my late grandmother Marie Shaw (Mama) and Aunt May for all of her wonderful prayers of agreement. To Aunt Debbie Shaw & Will and to the entire Shaw Family: Trina, Charnell, Tabrina, Tolia, Corey, Chantreea, Nettie, Tim, Tony, Joy, Lasheba, Sabrina, and to my brother in laws: David Cooper and Brian Cooper and to our friends of the immediate family

Ms. Rhonda Lyles and Steve and Ms. Hazel.

To my colleagues of OSU Barber College Daniel Crease, Terry Wade & Arthur Washington. A special recognition to my former co-workers: Ted Murdaugh, Jim Rulli, Ted Chrome, Ed Sr. & Bill Frazee, Thea Gatliff, Serena Crockett, Donald Peoples, and Christian rap artist D-Johnson.

To my spiritual mothers in the faith Clair Alston, Mary Towns, Ms. Banks, and Veronica Anthony thank you for all your prayers. Also, a special thank you and spiritual acknowledgement to my spiritual parents and mentors that help me developed from a spiritual infant to spiritual maturity in the faith in life's wonderful journey.

The late Elder Leroy Trout Sr. and late Elder Annie Shaw, the late Elder Charles Towns Sr. as well as my eternal prayer warrior partner the late Sister White. Also, to the first Pastor that ordained me as a minister Pastor William Craig of Christian Home Ministries Church, and to my other spiritual prayer band partners Sis. Jeanette Hawkins and Sis. Erma, plus Bishop Watkins, Bishop Timothy Clark, Pastor Kevin Burrows, for their spiritual teachings that help contribute to my spiritual development, because when I was a child, I spoke as a child; I understood as a child, I thought as a child: but when I became a man, I put away childish (and fleshly) things (1st Corinthians ch.13 verse 11).

Printed in the United States
By Bookmasters